Dedic
Munchy th

# A Long Lie Down

England to Morocco by
Vespa or C90.
Which will break down first?

by **Es Kaye**
with additional material by
**Nathan Statham**

First published as an over-priced photo book in 2010.
This edition 2023.
Cheapskate edition with no photos.

Copyright 2023 by the author of this book (Scott Kindleysides).
All photos taken by the author.
The book author retains sole copyright to all his contributions to this book.

This book is sold subject to the condition that it shall not, by way of trade of otherwise, be leant, re-soled, highered out or otherwise circulated without the authors consent in any form whatsoever.
In other words, watch out for el Turro.

This book is also available with photos:
A Long Lie Down with Photos

# 1

# First we need some transport

September 2009

## Breakdown

"YOU' RE mad".

"Wow"!

"Where are you going to break down? Do you mind if we start a sweepstake"?

These were a few things I first heard when I announced to my friends and family that I would ride my 36-year-old Vespa to Africa and back. But who cares about sanity when you have a vintage scooter and an itch for adventure? When most people talk about leaving everything behind to go on an adventure, they find too many excuses to stay behind. People would worry about their families, their houses, their job, how to pay the bills when they were away, etc. As for me, I did not have all those things to begin with so it was quite easy to pack a bag and head into the unknown without worrying about the consequences. In fact, I had done it quite often. I had saved as much money as possible from my poorly paid work to go travelling. To save money, I sacrificed a few things. I stopped going out, I avoided buying the latest phones and the coolest music and I didn't order too many take-aways. The more money I could save, the longer I could spend on holiday. That was enough encouragement for me.

And so the plan was set in motion. My good friend Kevin (Kev) would join me for most of the way. He was in a similar position to me, with little money and no important commitments that could stop him from going on an adventure.

The only travel preparation I made was to book a ferry which would take me and Kev off this tiny island and onto mainland Europe. That was the only thing that I had booked in advance for the entire journey. We would sail from Portsmouth, U.K. to Bilbao, Spain. I would ride my recently restored 1974 Vespa Rally 200. Kev would take his 1991 Honda C90 in his van, first to Portugal and then he would ride it from there to

Morocco.

# Break a leg

'Why was he not riding to Portugal?' you may ask... Well, he needed to go to Portugal to help a friend. That was a good enough reason for me to go for a ride on my scooter too, as I needed to go shopping for some Amlou paste (a kind of honey and almond paste which is delicious. I couldn't find it in Tesco). Well, I had an Italian shopping bike so I thought "Let's go shopping"!

To save some money, as we were on a very tight budget, we took the ferry to Bilbao in northern Spain, as opposed to riding through France, which we seriously debated but decided that would have been expensive. At that time, I wasn't entirely sure which route I would take for the return journey. Kev would probably stay in Portugal after the trip, so I would essentially be on my own.

Getting there is always the best and most exciting part of a trip, but coming home is not necessarily something to look forward to. But that wasn't important as yet. I would cross that sea when I came to it.

# Breakdance

Kev and I had talked about a trip like this many times in the past, especially after a few beers, so, it was time for action. No more talking. I had already been in the process of restoring a Vespa Rally 200 scooter, while Kev was in the process of restoring his liver. So, I had some transport and he had some transplant. That meant that he had stopped going down the pub and instead was saving money and on the lookout for a cheap Citroen 2CV or some form of very cheap transportation that was not designed for intercontinental travel. A small budget was the most important element.

We later found out that there was no such thing as a cheap Citroen 2CV as they were quite collectable.

OK. How about something cheaper? How about a motorbike? Honda C90? OK. That would do nicely.

# Shake your tail feather

A little later on, during the summery September month of 2009, we found out that Kev had the winning bid on a Honda Cub 90 which had been auctioned on eBay. After telling the seller our interstellar plan of riding it to Morocco, he kindly chucked (or should that be chuckled) in some waterproof clothing, a helmet, some gloves, spare tyres and tubes as well as a few good lucks.

Up to that time, Kev hadn't even passed his CBT - Compulsory Basic Training, which was required to get a motorbike licence. So, receiving all the extras was a great result.

## Watusi

I had most of the basics already as I owned other Italian shopping bikes including a 1966 SS180, 2 x ET3 and the recent box of bits I bought, called a Rally 200. I had owned the SS180 for the past 30 years and used it to travel around the country, where I would get drunk and listen to the coolest beats at the Mod rallies and all-nighters of the late 1980s and early 1990s.

Initially, I had planned to take one of my ET3s to Morocco and back but after I restored one of them, I then quickly sold it. When the buyer came to collect it, an Italian Vespa freak, he joked that the British mods and scooterists took all the small frame Vespas out of Italy in the 1980s and now they wanted them back! To add insult to injury he then saw the other ET3 I had, the one I had planned to take me on the journey to Africa. As he stood and admired the fact that it also still had the original toolbox and other 'Italian' features, he decided to commandeer it by immediately offering me a big handful of cool, hard cash. I could not have refused such an offer, so I sold it.

Now what would I do? I no longer had a ride. The vintage SS was not up for any long trips abroad. It was too old and demanded lots of attention to keep it mobile. It was of a different generation you see and did not like travelling too far from home, so could not be persuaded too easily.

## Willie and the Hand Jive

So as you should have guessed by now, I decided to take the box of bits - the Vespa Rally 200. But first, I had to finish rebuilding it so I could ride off into the sunset in search of adventure.

We planned to leave after eight weeks. These machines needed to be fully roadworthy.

# 2

## Have transport will travel

*November 2009*

WARNING! - For Vespa freaks only!

   Here are the boring bits/technical details about my Vespa. If you are not a Vespa freak, I would probably skip this part.

   It's a 1974 Vespa Rally 200. I bought this as a project a few months before I decided to go shopping in Morocco. The engine came as a box of bits. The bodywork had the usual rust and excessive filler typical of a 1970s Vespa. I wanted to preserve the original paintwork as much as possible as I had not intended to make it a show winner... I intended to ride it, not hide it. I quite like a bit of patina, but it was flaking off in between my fingers. The rust needed to be treated somehow. Lacquer was not going to work. I did not have any side panels either so they would not have matched up anyway.

I found an orange Hammerite type of paint - Rust-o-leum, made for farm machinery, snow ploughs and forklift trucks, etc., that I could use. The individual components of the Vespa were dismantled, cleaned, primed and given seven coats of the finest orange rust-preventative paint that money could buy. I applied it all with a small roller brush. Each coat was dried, sanded down and painted over again. It would at least match the Hammerite finish on all the silver components, such as the wheels and stand, etc.

I wanted to make it as original as possible, or at least make it look like it did when it rolled out of the Italian factory. Most of the parts in the box of bits were past their wear-by date, covered in rust or were not meant for that engine so I had no choice but to buy new parts. I was disappointed because I had hoped to do this on a small budget. Note to self: Vintage Vespas = not cheap. It was missing a few expensive components, like both side panels and major engine parts. I ended up getting one side panel from a dealer from Italy for an extortionate price. I remember collecting it from the dealer himself. I met him in a car park on the outskirts of town. He came direct from Italy in a large, fully loaded Mercedes Sprinter van, which was packed to the roof with 'barn finds' of classic Lambrettas and Vespas. As for the other panel, I had finally found one and I paid just 10% of the price I paid for the 'Italian import'! A big thanks to James for that.

But, no thanks go to the next guy…

## Nil Point

Due mainly to time constraints, I decided to let a 'professional' (I use that term loosely in this case) rebuild the engine. I wanted it to be totally standard as I knew way back when I bought it that I would probably want to ride it off this island.

Unfortunately, that monkey took a lot longer than anticipated to finish the engine.

And finish the engine he did.

It was no more.

It was deceased.

It was an ex-engine.

## Standard

I found out, all too late, that instead of fitting the standard gearbox I had bought and supplied him, the mechanic tried to fit the Vespa 150 Super gearbox which was part of the 'box of bits' collection. The engine functioned well enough to pass the MOT but failed soon after. The monkey never changed all of the bearings or seals, copper plumbing pipe was used to make the primary drive shaft fit and nothing was cleaned or inspected. It was as if he had waited until the 11th hour to rebuild it, then decided to assemble whichever parts he picked up first. Basically, he took an extremely long time to do a very bad job.

Since then, I decided to rebuild the engine myself. The engine now had the proper gearbox and I fitted a cosa clutch as the cheap copy I had, although new, just did not work too well.

I had rebuilt the entire scooter from scratch. Each and every component was thoroughly inspected with my own eyes and a set of callipers. If it was serviceable it was restored by hand and re-used. I figured parts back then were of better quality than those of today.

Another thing that was not standard for a 1974 Vespa Rally 200 was the upgraded 12-volt ignition although the lights were still rubbish but at least they would not attract too many insects. Originally it had the Femsa ignition system.

However, despite these setbacks, it was officially on

the road. I had all the paperwork and no longer had to worry about M.O.T. or road tax, or re-registration. After I had run it in, by riding 650 miles in 4 days, I discovered that I needed to change the 'new' main bearings!

Doh! What happened?

That was the only task the 'monkey' completed that I did not redo myself because I did not have the necessary equipment and I had very little time remaining before I set off. So, I found a highly recommended, well-reputed chap, who luckily lived quite local, to change all the bearings and seals for me and get it back to standard. Then all that was left to do would be to re-fit the engine. That all took a couple of weeks. During that time I had to work to further fund the trip.

In the meantime, I re-adjusted my original Madrid-style rear carrier that I had nicked off my SS180. I needed something to carry my tent, sleeping bag, clothes, etc. I got it to fit after I found a big hammer and a drill. No racks were harmed or killed during that procedure.

The next day I attempted the Front Carrier Manoeuvre. Which involved another assault on the SS180, this time stealing the front rack.

## Modifications

Kev had also been busy making a few alterations to his mean machine. Unlike me, he wanted to build a specimen that did not look like it had just rolled out of the showroom. There were a few things he didn't like about his bike, such as the very handy, functional and stylish top box and the map holder, which were the first things he disposed of.

Talking of maps, we did not take any maps. So actually the map holder would have been of no use. The rough plan, as it started to hatch, was to reach Spain, then head west and follow the coast south. If we had to, we could look at the miniature maps in a Rough Guide book I had. However, as it turned out, Kev did not like guidebooks either and cunningly forgot to bring them on the trip.

I did however carry a small Nokia phone, screen size 2" or something crazy. It had a map on it which turned out to be pretty rubbish. I tried it once, my first time following a GPS signal. I followed it round and round a roundabout then decided I would just "keep straight for the next 124 km", and not look at it any more.

## Rocker Vacations

I was not entirely sure exactly what modifications had been carried out on the C90 but I knew he had talked excitedly about fitting the following;

a different exhaust,

2 x storage boxes bolted onto the rear,

a high-performance air filter,

go faster stripes,

new tyres and most importantly, an extremely loud horn taken off the Royal Enfield that Kev drove around India. I was jealous. His horn was bigger than mine.

## The Oil Slik Road

As for the Vespa...

A few days before we were due to depart from Portsmouth, I went with a couple of mates to collect another engine for the Vespa. A well-used Spanish P200 motor. I hoped it was looking forward to returning home soon. Thanks go to Dr Venturi and Satnav Paul for their help.

So why did I need another engine? The scooter was OK, wasn't it? The original engine was being rebuilt by a well-reputed mechanic, wasn't it? Well, it was yes, but the 'new' mechanic noticed that the bearings had been spinning in the crankcases, the crank threads were stripped, the stator plate was cracked, etc. This was noticed just a few days before we were due to leave. Those were the new parts I had supplied to the monkey.

Ideally, it would be easier to find another engine. As if I could find another engine just four days before the trip. It was not something I could just buy off the shelf or had the money to do so. I had already spent most of my hard-earned bucks on spare engine parts. This all meant that I would be using a second-hand Spanish Vespa P200 engine that I had just bought at a parts fair. It would slot straight into my scooter since it was simply an upgraded version of the original engine.

Most of the problems I had with the original Rally engine were due to the monkey I let loose on it, who attempted to install incompatible parts while blindfolded. I could mention his name but my left eye still develops a nervous twitch every time it's mentioned.

## Chutney

So, after miraculously finding a replacement engine, I gave the 'new' old engine a much-needed clean at the local jet wash, using a trowel to scrape off the thick layer of accumulated Spanish oil and dirt.

Underneath all this was a fairly clean-looking engine and just like its new owner, it scrubbed up quite well. All that was needed was to swap the new parts I had already bought for the original engine, like the gears, cylinder, carburettor (carb') etc and replace the bearings and seals and give it a test ride. To do that, I took it back to the same local mechanic, who was once again, very kindly willing to drop everything after I told him my latest predicament. I had seriously thought about doing it myself but I did not have the time, even though my tool kit started to expand as I progressed through the failures.

# 3

## Engines

### Decided

There were only four more days remaining before we would catch the ferry. That left us little time to prepare. Kev and I had a rough plan which developed further as the days were counted down. We had also been busy at work so that we could actually pay for our elaborate adventure. Up to that point in time, there hadn't been much action. With the exception of riding around and destroying 2 x engines of course.

I had received the 'new' old Spanish engine back and had done a few hundred miles running it in, as it had new bearings and seals, etc., fitted. I went on a 200 km round trip to get some fish and chips which seemed like a good way to break in the newly built motor. I also gave it a couple of trips up and down the M11 motorway, just to give it a 'real' test. It was always an unknown, breaking in a new engine on a motorway. I had to be confident nothing untoward would happen on the test run as if it broke down on the motorway, it would have made the return journey home extremely difficult. There would likely be no convenient lay-bys/houses/garages/cafes/etc., to sit in and wait for assistance or attempt a repair.

That old Spanish engine was nowhere near as fast as the previous, standard Rally 200 engine (when it was running). I got a top speed of just below 60 mph if I was lucky. I was reassured by the mechanic that it was typical for an old P200.

Thanks, btw, go to Antony at Buzzsolomoto for getting me another engine when I needed one fast and thanks to the mechanic who did another super fast rebuild for me but nicked all the expensive new parts I originally bought. I was threatened with violence if I insisted that they were actually mine. That's why this engine was so slow. I would never trust another mechanic again.

## Delagered

The few remaining days before our adventure

began, Kev had to take his CBT (Compulsory Basic Training for motorcycles). As he took the test on his C90 he had to re-fit a few things to make it 'legal' again, such as the; leg shields, new exhaust and 'L'oser plates. A new K and N air filter was also fitted, in the hope it would make the C90 faster. After a quick tune-up by 2-stroke wizard, Dr. Simon Venturi, it was ready for the test the following day.

Kev (and Dr. Venturi) passed their CBT, which meant Kev was legally on the road, probably for the first time ever.

To get used to the bike, he released the 10-year-old inside of him into the wild and as such he was spotted ripping up the tarmac, doing doughnuts in the dark, wheelying into wheelie bins, hitting potholes, going the wrong way up a one-way street and racing dogs. He was ready for adventure!

After a few more tweaks to the clutch and indicators, Kev took off the legshields once more, He adjusted a few more bits and bobs, gave a satisfied smile and an all-knowing nod. He was now the proud owner of a newly created life. It was christened, "Munchy the Crunchy" - Munchy because it munched away at his wallet and Crunchy because a C90 is also known as a crunchy (it's a semi-automatic - you crunch the gears into place with no clutch lever). With the addition of one Kev, everything would be set to go.

## On the wagon

Being afraid that Kev's bike was going to be faster than mine, I had also been playing with my Vespa. With the 'new' old engine fitted, I had hoped to make it as fast as possible. But, I found out that the later Spanish P200 engines were more restricted than earlier Rally 200 engines. Allegedly. I personally think it was because old, worn parts had been re-fitted and the new parts had been pocketed by the mechanic.

So, as I wanted my machine to go that little bit faster too, and like most Vespa enthusiasts, I went ahead with a not-thoroughly-thought-through-idea, and with bad advice, I decided to change the carburettor. It was not a difficult process. I then took the scooter for another test ride with great expectations. Yet 20 metres outside my home, it died suddenly.

It seized.

It was deceased.

It was no more.

## A.A.

What had happened? It was a newly rebuilt engine! I pushed it all the way home, 20 whole metres, with my head held low.

After I pulled the engine apart, I discovered that a vagrant washer from the carburettor had managed to lodge its way in between the crankcase sealing pad and the crankshaft, which made a nice snug home for itself, without paying any rent, and as a result, it ended up seizing the crank. Maybe even destroying the crankcase sealing pad, which would have rendered the whole engine unusable.

There was no time to cry. After a thorough inspection, I decided the engine cases were OK. But, I had to take a quick 450 km round trip to Beedspeed in Grimsby for some spares - a new crank, as the previous one was twisted. I also bought new bearings and seals (again).

I decided that there would be no more monkeying around rebuilding the engine and did all the work myself. There was simply no more time to galavant around the country searching for spares and thieving, monkey mechanics.

As I still had to squeeze in some work during the day before I left, most of the engine rebuild was successfully carried out late at night, in a tiny wooden shed, on the floor, in the dark, with a torch.

All that was left to do was to take it for another long test run the next day to find out if it could make it to Northern Africa the following day.

## Snakebite and Black

I originally started this blog with the heading 'Vespa or C90, which will break down first?'

I should have written, 'C90 or Vespa, which will be ready first?'

I thought my Vespa project would be simple enough. All I wanted was a standard bullet-proof Vespa Rally 200 engine in a standard Vespa Rally 200 frame and to ride it to Morocco. And of course, back again. I kept forgetting that bit. Not much to ask, was it?

Hopefully, having all these problems at 'home' would mean I wouldn't get any when I would be 'on the road'.

On the positive side, the optional extras I had fitted worked well; a 12-volt battery to power 2 x 'wind tone' horns (in retaliation to Kev's big horn) and a cigarette lighter socket to charge my mobile phone, which were both fully functional. A big, loud horn is a must in any country if you're on a small bike. Sometimes more important than good brakes!

## Cocktail

For the final time, just before departure day arrived, Kev and I went out on the road together. I was surprised by just how fast the C90 was. I was also surprised by just how slow the Vespa was. How could a stylish Italian, with 200cc, the power of 10 horses, and a top speed of a leopard, fail to convincingly annihilate a Japanese classic with only 90cc, 7 horses and a top speed that was slower than a Hummingbird? I guess it was an age thing. The Vespa was much older.

Thankfully for me, my little, orange scooter was still just a little faster than Munchy. I could just keep up with the C90 when I was going flat out in 3rd gear although when I changed into 4th gear there wasn't much more top speed available. Still, it gave me just enough power to sloooowly creep by Kev, read all the slogans on the stickers which adorned the rear side racks on the Honda, look at his speedo, see how fast he was going, grin, give him the finger and eventually overtake him. I never looked back. I was too busy laughing.

Feeling a little jealous, and wanting more power, Kev decided to fit a larger front sprocket to his C90. That made me a little nervous, as I thought it would make the C90 a little faster but we were yet to find out as we had almost run out of preparation time.

# Tom Cruise

Exactly what I ended up taking depended on how much stuff would fit into my bag. I preferred to travel light, so, I did what I had always done when venturing to another country - I laid out everything I wanted to take with me on my bed and then got rid of half of it.

I packed everything I planned to take, loaded it all onto the scooter and took it for another test ride. Everything included things such as; a tent, sleeping bag, small mattress, clothes, etc. I did not take many big spares but I did pack a comprehensive tool kit that fitted nicely into a small wash bag and was stored in my toolbox, along with a spare 2 litres of fuel, 2T (2-stroke) oil and a 'rainproof' poncho. As I travelled light, rather than taking more spare tyres and wheels and tubes, I packed a puncture repair kit and a tiny foot pump.

## Mission Impossible

Before the trip, many people had asked us,
"Where are you going exactly"?
"What's the plan"?
"Why don't you just fly"?
We finally had a confirmed answer - We were going to Morocco via Spain and Portugal. Here's the updated plan we had:

I planned to ride my scooter all the way to Marrakesh, Morocco and back, from Diss, Norfolk, U.K. Kev planned to drive his van to Portugal with the C90 loaded in the back and then from there, we both planned to ride our 2-wheelers together via Portugal and Spain, to various places in Morocco such as Marrakesh, Essaouira, Casablanca, the Sahara, etc.

# Cunning plan

The first part of the trip would take me from Diss to Portsmouth, to catch the ferry to Bilbao, Spain. I barely thought about that part of the trip, as I felt like it would be a walk in the park. I had even planned to briefly stop on the way, to stock up on spares and grab a cup of tea from the legends at Allstyles Scooters. But that depended on my scooter's performance and the time it would take to complete the Diss - Portsmouth leg of the journey.

And then? What was the plan? Well, after a 2-day boat journey, we would arrive in Bilbao where we would head west and follow the coast until we reached Portugal. From there, we would take a few days to travel along the Portuguese coastline, to eventually end up in the Algarve in southern Portugal. We would stay there for a week or two to rest and further prepare Kev's C90 for the beginning of his two-wheeled adventure.

And then? And then we would both ride towards Algeciras in Spain to catch the ferry to Morocco.

## Punning clan

And then?
And then ride around Morocco until;

a) our money runs out
b) our petrol runs out
c) our puns run out
d) our patience runs out

# 4

## 2 days to go

## Ready

We were almost ready. The machines were also just about ready for adventure.

Kev's C90 had a new lightweight front mudguard which effortlessly painted a perfectly straight line of murky road water onto his face. The leg shields had been removed and bulletproof rear carriers were added, along with new indicators and a new paint job. All in all, it was a superb all-terrain vehicle.

## Steady

The Vespa was finally ready to go. In the 2 months leading up to my departure, it had had;

2 x engines,

4 x engine rebuilds,

1 x seizure

2 x new cranks and

1 x puncture

Most of these setbacks were because I and some other monkeys didn't know what we were doing during the 'restoration'.

It also had a rear carrier fitted (from the SS180). I added Goop, a puncture preventative to my tyres as I was prone to the odd puncture. I couldn't say for sure if the Goop actually prevented any punctures but I never had any trouble with such things ever since.

## Go!

It was interesting to see what and how much we could load onto these machines. Although I preferred the minimalist approach, in previous lives while riding Vespas around the world, I had managed to transport things such as; three adults with their weekly shopping, a big bank of lorry batteries with gas bottles, a brood of chickens and a live goat and countless passengers. No, not all at once I must add as that was just a little bit more than the law would allow.

## Cheggers Plays Pop

I didn't have much experience with C90's so, I didn't know exactly what they were capable of but I believed anything was possible. I also truly believed both of these machines were capable of going anywhere other bikes could go. It all depended on the riders' skill, judgement and sheer stupidity, as to exactly how far and where they could actually go.

## Runaround

We were pretty much set, and ready for adventure.

# 5

# And we were off

## Fiddle Sticks

After literally minutes and minutes of planning the whole trip, and after hours, days and months of restoring, redesigning and re-repairing our vehicles, the day finally came when we were ready to leave behind our comfortable beds and depart for adventure.

## Weather Sticks

We left the safety and comfort of our homes and began the journey from Diss to Portsmouth at around 9 in the morning. While driving in the comfort of his van, Kev smoked about 100 fags while watching me getting blown around like a fly trapped inside a vacuum cleaner. Head-on winds meant I had cruising speeds of just 40 - 50 mph, with a maximum of 60 mph in the slipstream of passing lorries. It turned out that the day we set off, according to the Met Office, was the wettest since records began way back in 1911.

The Vespa suffered from just one problem which was the rear light bulb had blown (due only to it not being seated correctly in the holder). After I changed it, it was never a problem ever again. I was quite pleased with my electrical skills as I had designed, made and fitted the new and upgraded wiring loom myself. Mr. Piaggio did not include phone chargers in his initial draughts of the Rally 200. I never did make it to Allstyles for that cup of tea, I did not have time, due to the ridiculous

weather I had experienced that particular day.

# Temple Balls

When we finally arrived at the ferry terminal in Portsmouth at 3:45 pm, we sat and had a coffee and waited to board the ferry. I started to make a 'rolly', a handmade cigarette, then discovered I had bought with me the wrong pouch of tobacco. The pouch I had grabbed on my way out of the house when I left was in fact full of some other substance that would not be good to have on you when you go through a customs checkpoint. It was a substance that resembled 'Nepali Temple Ball'. I did not want to throw it away as it was rare and expensive, so I ended up posting *most* of it back home.

At the terminal, waiting to board the ferry, we loaded the Vespa into Kev's van for the sea crossing (purely to save money on the tickets). Kev then reminded me that he, "always gets stopped by Customs", because he had an old, slightly beaten up van, with discarded cigarette boxes, Rizla papers, etc., on the dashboard behind the front window screen, for everyone to see. I should add that he is not a toker.

Anyway, we only just managed to fit the scooter

inside and it caused a bit of a scene in doing so. It looked like it would fit easily but that was just an illusion.

After we finally managed to squeeze it in without breaking anything a customs official came over to inspect everything...

"Alright boys"? he asked in a knowing way.

"Yeh, sure. Go away. Nothing to see here", I thought to myself.

We told him about our plans to go to Morocco on the two shopping bikes he could see in the back of the van. He looked confused. Did he hear that correctly? He looked back over his shoulder admiringly at a couple of other big boys', proper motorcycles that were getting ready to depart these shores all fully kitted out with expensive saddlebags, side racks, off-road tyres, GPS systems, windshields, heated grips, etc.

## Red Leb'

It did not look good for us. For a moment, the clipboard he was holding, along with the hi-viz jacket he was wearing, seemed to have given him some extra special powers and he looked ready to strip search the van. Us too probably. But the gods were on our side and he must have decided that we were just a couple of innocent idiots who had no idea of how underprepared we were. So after looking back again at the well-prepared bikes, he decided to teach us a lesson by letting us go and try riding these silly little bikes to Africa. And so, he waved us on with a look that suggested he wanted us to fail. For a moment I thought I would end up in a very different place. It really could have potentially been the end of the trip but we were finally on the ferry. Our feet were no longer touching this tiny little island and were ready to lead us to the unknown. I checked my Temple Balls and waved goodbye to Blighty.

## Yellow Leb'

Once we were settled into our chairs and ready for the 30 hour journey on the ferry, we let Robbie Villiams entertain us. That could have been the reason for the gale-force winds and heavy rain that still followed our every move so far. So, it was time to get spannered and dream of what was going to happen when we got off the ferry. I started to ask myself stupid questions like, will the Vespa make it? Did I save enough money to reach home again? Did I pack enough spares? I was not talking about underpants either. If you're wondering, I travel light. I took 3 pairs. One pair to fool them all, one pair to mind them, one pair to wash them all, and in the darkness find them.

## Red Leb'

Who was going to break down first? My main concern was that if my scooter was going to break down in Morocco, how would I fix it or more importantly, how would I get home? Or even more importantly, how would I get the Vespa home? It was a big investment as it was a classic model and well sought after. It meant that it was quite collectable and valuable. It was not something I could easily replace and neither was it something I wanted to replace. When I first bought the box of bits, I intended to use it

as my main vehicle for the next few years, not just for an adventurous shopping trip. Ride it, not hide it. And btw, I decided to name it as a genderless -
"The Vespa " - an adventurous, attractive head-turner that was surprisingly strong.

# Yellow Leb'

Robbie Villiams had stopped entertaining me and the boat had stopped moving. It had finally arrived at Bilbao. After reaching mainland Europe we headed west along the coast. It was good to be back on The Vespa again. The first place we camped was at a small campsite in Luarco, Spain. The following morning, we woke up to gorgeous sunshine rising over the town below, which was a big relief as there was no rain. I was still smiling.

It all seemed so surreal to be there, on The Vespa, which just a few days before was laid on its side in my cold and damp garden in England, undergoing major surgery, not knowing if it was going to survive. It was a feeling of relief for me. There was no going back. I felt glad to be alive and to be in sunny Spain.

## Manala Cream

After I packed my tent, etc., (Kev slept in his van) we followed the coast around the Bay of Biscay, and as we went through the ancient towns and villages we unintentionally visited the second-highest town in the province. As I slowly rode uphill through the centre, going slower and slower as the hill got steeper and steeper, I noticed lots of people outside small restaurants.

They were cooking what appeared to be octopus with red wine in a large pot. We were both hungry and feeling adventurous, so with high spirits we decided to stop there for breakfast. The first few mouthfuls were quite enjoyable but it was a bit too much for my inexperienced taste buds at that time in the morning.

## Charas

During the day, our second in Spain, we spent our time going up and down more mountain roads, in fresh, heavy rain and extra strong winds. Going down some of those long hills on an air-cooled 2-stroke was a little frightening because to keep the fuel flowing, which helps keep the piston cool, I had to give it more throttle, which in turn made it go faster. And those hills were long. Halfway down a hill, and hanging on for dear life, my speedometer needle began to reach its limits. So did my underpants. I tried to help the situation by using my 'air-brakes' - by sitting bolt upright, with my elbows and knees bent outwards and creating as much wind resistance as possible.

## Blow-back

The wind was so strong that it tried to steal my helmet and strangled me. The rain was so heavy that it pushed my face into the speedometer. I could barely see where I was going. It was like taking a shower in a convertible car, in a carwash, on a fishing trawler, in the middle of the Atlantic Ocean with only a paper napkin to keep me dry.

I always rode with an open-faced helmet, so my face had little protection from the elements, the rain stinging my face every time the skies opened up. When was it ever going to stop following us?

And all the time Kev was in the comfort of his van. His nice, warm, comfortable van I kept thinking to myself. Actually, the wind and rain were an exhilarating experience. I did not mind getting wet and blown around. It reminded me of when I was much younger and even more carefree. A time of riding scooters around the U.K., sometimes with friends, where we would secretly mock anyone who wore any type of waterproof clothing, whereas we only wore Jeans, T-shirts, desert boots and sunglasses. Maybe a jacket if it was snowing! Only joking.

## Blow Up

Later in the day, while going downhill my scooter soft-seized. I had no idea why. Nothing had changed in the last 2000 km or so. I put it down to the semi-synthetic 2-stroke oil I was using (which was recommended by the light-fingered mechanic No. 2). In my mind, using semi-synthetic oil was like admitting that you did not know which oil is best, synthetic or mineral, so use them both.

After holding up the traffic on the way there, we

found another campsite and in the small office space was a little blue, small door, small frame Vespa. In great condition too. My offer of 250 Euros was enough for the owner to produce yet another bottle of his own wine, but not enough to buy the small door.

## One Mint Julep

I spent the next day getting wet but at least I had a different view this time which helped relieve the hangover. As we travelled through the rain, heads slightly dizzy, we made it to our next stop, Porto, Portugal which was also great because they had some nice, cheap beer, Sagres - cheapest and the best. On the way, Kev was delighted as he decided to get his bike, Munchy the Crunchy, out of the van and on the road for a little jaunt around the area. We took a quick day trip to the highest peak we could find which had great views of the River Lima below. The winding roads with narrow, sharp corners were all a good test for Kev and I, and our bikes. Later that day we ate more seafood, slept well and dreamt of Africa.

## Duas cervejas

Another campsite, another beer and another hangover later, we found ourselves in Lisbon. I did not recall stopping long. I think Kev was bored with following me on The Vespa all the way from our home town to southern Portugal so when he recognized a road he had travelled on before, he finally took the lead and drove as fast as he possibly could on the windy, twisty roads of Faro district, trying to lose The Vespa. But to no avail, as thankfully, I was always able to catch up with him. I say thankfully because we were heading for his friend's house in the Algarve somewhere and I had no clue as to exactly where that somewhere was. I do not think he wanted to tell either. I think he just wanted to create some mischief to relieve the boredom he had been suffering in the van.

## And a packet of crisps, please

The Vespa was doing OK. I rode it everywhere as

fast as the brakes would allow. Kev was in front of me for the first time during the trip. I guessed the plan had changed. There would be no more coastal roads. The mission was on, to reach our destination before sunset. No more slowly meandering along the coast or through the countryside and mountains. It was time to see if The Vespa, a Rally 200, could actually live up to its name and survive a small rally in the Algarve.

# 6

# Bon Dias

## Destination

We reached our first planned destination of Luz de Tavira near Faro on the southern coast of Portugal in the evening, just before sunset.

There was a headwind all the way down to the Algarve except for one day when we had some sunshine. The rain, gale-force winds, etc., had followed us all the way here from home.

When we arrived in Luz and found a bar, the locals told us it was the first rain they had seen for months. That was a blessing for the many orange farmers nearby. They actually thanked us for bringing the rain, and I was really thrilled to give it to them too. I had been wet enough times already. At least it was warmer there. I could dry my clothes pretty quickly. We experienced T-shirt weather during the days and cooked on open, outdoor fires in the evenings. It was time to relax and burn some sausages.

## Moo Moo land

Overall, we took a leisurely four days to get there, leaving at around 10 am each day and setting up camp at around 4 pm - 5 pm. Nothing too strenuous. We were having a long lie down after all.

We had completed almost 2000 km up to that point. (Kilometres sound more impressive than miles). So were there any problems on the way down I hear you ask?

Let's start with The Vespa - apart from changing the rear bulb, I experienced a bird hitting me in the face. I was going so fast on my Vespa that it could not get out of the way quickly enough.

Kev's old van, which was also on the list of endangered vehicles that was potentially going to break down, was also going well. Nothing to report except a dodgy wire in the brake light. Similar to The

Vespa.

However, Kev's C90, which he barely rode in the last 2000 km, had suffered the worst damage - a broken indicator, while it was in the back of his van. That was very likely due to his need for speed the day before when he raced to Luz. He soon fixed the indicator with sticky tape and tested extensively by doing a few wheelies on a deserted road.

## Justified

We stayed in a small villa, surrounded by fruiting orange trees which was owned by a friend of Kev's. Kev's main reason for going to Portugal in the first place was to help his friend renovate his house. That plan then evolved into me joining him where I would continue on to Africa on a Vespa to get the Amlou paste, which I had almost forgotten about.

For me, this still seemed like it was only the start of the trip. It seemed too easy up to that point, despite the horrendous weather. But, with the feeling of not having to work and having the freedom to go wherever I wanted, I began to embrace the wind and rain. It did not matter. Nothing mattered.

If Aum was the vibration that gave power to the universe then 'wwhhhhhhrrrrr' was the vibration that ran through my body and powered my journey, as The Vespa tunefully escorted me to yet another unknown place.

I figured I had enough money to last me at least a couple of months, hopefully, longer. But I intended to make this trip last as long as possible and with no rush.

We stayed in Luz for a couple of weeks. During that time, we enjoyed a local diet of fish and beer as well as exploring the area. Kev could then concentrate on his bike, getting it into shape for, what was for me, the beginning of the start of the adventure.

Meanwhile, Kev had been busy checking all the screws would loosen and tighten back up correctly. He also added extra embellishments to his C90. I had kept busy by doing nothing and chillin' some more.

## Ancient

All in all, we were in good spirits.

# 7

## Let the games commence

## Fun

So far on this journey, nothing of much significance had happened to me, Kev, his van or The Vespa. Much to the dismay of the non-believers.

On The Vespa, I had travelled over 2000 km, averaging around 333 km a day, riding for about 4 or 5 hours a day, pretty comfortably. Likewise with Kev, who was very comfortable in his nice warm van, listening to his stereo, smoking tabs and that. But, with Kev ditching his warm van in Luz, Portugal and finally getting on his C90, things started to get a little more interesting.

## Games

In Luz, where we stayed for a week or so, Kev transformed the kitchen into a motorbike workshop and had his C90 up on a makeshift platform to prepare his bike, just like a pro. His fingers were like magnets attracting the various tools laying around on the makeshift workbench, feverishly trying to fit anything that would make Munchy the Crunchy go faster.

Modifications included; changing the oil three times, stripping the carburettor a few times, and fitting a grill on the headlight which he later decided to take off just before we departed. Luckily for Kev, there was also another Honda C90 at the villa This ended up being used for spares. It once belonged to a friend named Tom who had planned to use it to set off from John O' Groats to Lands End. I think Kev was hoping to gain some of the essence from another well-travelled C90 and pass it on to Munchy by using some kind of mechanical voodoo involving some sticky tape, a hammer and a few carefully chosen magic words that described his frustration.

## Olympic

After Kev had cast his spell on Munchy, I also decided to get my scooter up on the platform to change the oil and prepare it. I would say it was well and truly run-in by now so it meant it was due for a service. I changed the oil, greased and oiled a few parts, and checked the nuts and bolts were all tight etc., which they were. Just regular service stuff. I did not know what else to do with it as it was running fine. I did however wipe off most of the bugs that were splattered across the front leg shield. That was about it. But, annoyingly, I ended up bending the front mudguard when it slipped off Kev's makeshift platform. I was annoyed that it
happened to my lovingly restored Rally 200 but this was probably the first of many knocks and scrapes to come. Never mind, I thought. I bought it to ride it. The damage, along with the bugs would add to the patina effect I was hoping to create and would always serve as a memory of that day.

After a few more days sitting around doing very little, I caught the tinkering bug and decided to clean the cylinder head and piston, which I found out was built up with carbon. Yes! I had done something useful to The Vespa. I had also off-set some carbon. It was a little nerve-racking, pulling apart an engine that did not really need fixing, especially when I was so far from home but it gave me more confidence in The Vespa and myself.

## Marathon

The fun and games commenced when we left for Morocco. I was still on the trusty Vespa with Kev finally joining me on his Honda C90, named "Munchy the Crunchy". I was not sure if Munchy was a boy or a girl. Either way, he paid a lot of attention to it. We both set off for Morocco on 2 wheels. Spain was only about 30 km from where we were staying in Portugal so we aimed to get at least to the other side of Sevilla just 180 km away. If the going was good, we would head straight for the ferry at Algeciras, which was for me, not an overly-ambitious 400 km away.

I thought, "We could do that in a day".

The Vespa was running OK. The weather changed for the better and Munchy the Crunchy was a bulletproof C90. Apparently, a P200 engine was also bulletproof. What could possibly happen?

## Munchies

We left Luz de Tavira in Portugal at 12 pm on 3rd December 2009.
Travelling such a short distance to reach another country would seem like a walk in the park compared to what we had just accomplished so we were both full of confidence. But after only 50 km, just across the border in Spain, about 1 hour into what I would define as the start of the trip, I thought it had ended.
I pulled over on the side of the road to see Kev with his tool kit out, holding a screwdriver and shaking his head.

"Oh, dear. So soon already"? I thought.

His well-maintained carburettor kept coming loose and was leaking petrol over his jeans and the spark plug if he went over 70 km/h. But, we soon got going again and made our way towards Seville. The Vespa did not enjoy travelling at 70 km/h on fast roads, so I raced ahead of Kev whenever we went uphill and I let him overtake me when we went downhill.

## C.H.i.P.s

A few kilometres before Seville however he did not overtake me. So I waited... and I waited… and I waited... Hmmm? He could not have been that far behind but I did not see him anywhere. I could not turn back either as we were on a one-way, 4-lane highway. I think his carburettor must have been playing up again. I had to keep moving as we were on a motorway as those Spanish motorcycle cops I had spotted earlier looked like they needed some money to buy their kids Christmas presents. So I carried on at a very slow pace, trying to make myself invisible to Poncho and Jono, the Spanish Highway Patrol.

## Monkey Magic

Maybe Kev did have some magic tricks up his sleeve after all. He had made himself invisible. I did not notice any roads off the highway that led to where we were going so surely he had to pass me soon. I had little option but to carry on slowly, hoping that Kev would come whizzing past me at some point in the day, waving his middle finger in delight. But no.

We both knew which road to take so I followed that route and it slowly began to sink in that we would not make it to Africa in a day.

# 8

# Honda C90...Bulletproof? My arse!

It may have been December by now. Who knows?

## Bullet

So what happened to Kev? Where did he go?

Let's imagine the voice of Kev.

"I was going slow uphill so Scott could keep up and fast downhill so Scott could not keep up, ha!ha!ha! But then I realised that the petrol gauge was going down quicker than I was moving. I looked down and noticed petrol leaking down my leg and over the spark plug. I pulled over, had a fag, tightened up the screws on the carb' again then realised I'd left the Locktite with the guide book".

He continued, "So, I carried on for another 10km. Scott had no mirrors, which is weird for an Italian hair dryer, so he didn't notice me on the side of the motorway fixing my carburettor and he went ahead without me".

So where did he go exactly?

"I took a detour to a national park as I was bored with the motorway and waited for Scott", he explained.

I think what he means is - he got lost. On the motorway.

## Trigger

Meanwhile, as I slowly rode along the freeway, waiting for Kev to catch up, my invisibility shield had worn off and I was pulled over by the Spanish Highway Patrol. I had been warned about those guys. They would take all your money and your children if your motorbike was not perfecto. They wanted to fine me 180 Euros as I did not have the two mandatory mirrors on The Vespa that they said were required by law. That was their excuse anyway. They refused to talk or understand English. Hey, not all Vespas have mirrors I thought to myself. I think they were jealous that everyone was looking at my scooter and not at their moustachios.

The two cops giggled in Spanish to each other as they thought of what to write on their On-the-spot-fine notepad/Xmas wish list.

I managed to explain in my best Spanglish that The Vespa had no mirrors when it was made some 36 years ago.

"Manufacturer no fabricado", I shouted proudly in my best Spanish accent, whilst pointing confidently to The Vespa.

They carefully touched their way around the legshields looking for some kind of evidence of a mirror but they found nothing. I prayed that they did not look under the handlebars, the standard place for a mirror bracket on a Vespa. I somehow managed to explain that I had ridden the Vespa the entire way from the U.K., through Portugal and Spain and I was on my way to Algeciras, without mirrors (or spotlights or a whippy aerial). That made them laugh even more and they just had to let me go.

So, I left them there laughing together and made a hasty getaway before they changed their minds and I headed to the nearest town to wait for Kev. As I arrived in Palace y Villafranca, a crazy bus driver kept overtaking me and pointing at me and The Vespa. He was grinning like a Spanish motorbike cop on laughing gas. I stopped to see what the excitement was about and found out he was another Vespa freak and owned one or two Vespas himself. Again, my lack of Spanish prevented me from fully communicating but I could clearly tell he was happy to see The Vespa. After a quick coffee, I asked him if he could recommend a cheap hotel. He then led me to a place in town, where later, after a couple of hours, I miraculously met up with Kev again. What a stroke of luck. Or was it magic? He had re-appeared! His magic tricks were pretty good!

I took my time to enjoy the new scenery and relaxed whilst Kev spent the evening preparing his bike some more. I awoke the following morning to eventually find Kev in the hotel basement, fixing his carb' yet again. He may have been there all night for all I know, beavering away like Rumpelstiltskin. This time he used Loctite adhesive that he managed to find in town. We then departed Villafranca and set off again - a day behind my imaginary schedule. But it didn't matter. Nothing was booked. We had lots of time to reach Algeciras and catch whichever ferry was available.

## Happy

On the way, we stopped for breakfast at a small cafe. The owner seemed excited to see us. I thought he may have been another Vespa freak but actually, I think he was smiling at our wallets. After we had finished eating, I pulled out a 20 Euro note to pay, expecting lots of change in return, but the owner took the lot. After he saw the surprised, dismayed and half-angry look on my face, he must have felt guilty and then gave us a "free" shot glass full of green liquid. It looked like washing detergent. Maybe it was Absinthe. We necked it anyway and left.

We continued towards Algeciras to catch the ferry to Morocco. Kev was listening to drum 'n' bass on his MP3 player and then realised it was not drum 'n' bass at all but his engine banging and knocking.

On the way, we got split up again in Jerez de la Frontera. Kev did his David Blaine vanishing act again. He was literally about 50 metres behind me, at the bottom of a hill, in traffic, waiting to merge onto another bigger, busier road. I slowly inched towards the main road and just as I was about to pull out and ride off into the sunset I noticed Kev..... No wait. I did not notice Kev. He had gone. Vanished. So I quickly pulled over to the side and looked up for a U.F.O. in the sky, thinking he may have been abducted by aliens in the blink of an eye.

# TV

I waited...and waited...this time I could turn back to find him, which I did but his trick was so good that he had completely vanished, even though what felt like just two seconds ago, he was right behind me. His close-up work was amazing. After searching high and low I could not find him. So what did I do? I headed off without him. Towards the road, we agreed to travel on beforehand. Again.

I continued on the bigger main road, which I later found out Kev was not allowed on, as his bike was considered a toy and not fit for fast roads such as these. I waited at a busy cafe where after one or two hours, Kev pulled up with his C90 banging away like a panel beater on amphetamines. He had to take the back roads reserved for gypsies riding donkeys where he says (and I do not believe a word of it) that he saw "...lots of people fixing Vespas on the roadside". This was his metaphor for "I broke down again".

## The Day Today

The original plan when we left the hotel that morning was to head straight for Algeciras. The same as it was on the first day of our 2 wheeled adventure together.

So, as we could not travel on normal roads we had a choice at the crossroads where we stood - Follow the old peasants' road towards Algeciras, which should be more scenic but slower, or take a different road that had a couple of towns on it where we could potentially find a hotel if we did not make it to the ferry.

In true professional explorer style, we tossed a coin to decide which road we would take. We ended up in a great little town by the name of Alcala de los Gazules and decided to stay there that night. It had taken us two days to travel about 100km. We asked an extremely helpful local by the name of Juanma if he knew of any cheap hotels in town. Many thanks go to Juanma for his expert and detailed knowledge, guided tour and his friendship in this popular hilltop town. It would have been nice to stay a little longer as it was such a quaint place but we wanted to catch that elusive ferry.

I persuaded Kev that he should forget about the banging and knocking engine for the time being and at least limp the final 60 km to Algeciras so we could get on the ferry and make it to Morocco, to prove all the non-believers wrong.

## The Bureau

And, that's exactly what we did. It took a couple of hours to travel those last few kilometres but we made it onto the ferry and arrived in Ceuta at around 2 pm that day. Ceuta is a tax-free Spanish province, so it was another 3 or 4 km to the actual Moroccan border and a further 100km to our planned destination of Chefchouean in the Rif mountains of northern Africa. It was also a fine opportunity to fill up with tax-free petrol. All 8-litres worth.

# 9

# You can't come in

## Bedlam

At the actual Moroccan border, we could tell immediately that we were no longer in Europe and on a different continent. It had the similar hustle and bustle of some of the Asian countries we had both visited before in previous lives. Much different to the slow-paced life of Spain and Portugal.

It was Bedlam. We could hear languages we did not understand. We did not know what the crack was to get through the border without getting ripped off, which was not so good.

Empty forms to fill in were shoved in our faces.

"Park bikes here",

"No, move them here",

"No move them here".

There were guys clutching documents, telling us we needed to fill them in, then insisting that they fill them in for us. Of course, they were going to ask for a small fee to 'help' us. So me being me, I wanted to do this myself and tried to ignore them all.

Meanwhile, Kev had a few guys helping him fill in his details. After getting a laser to the head from the medic to check for fever, I handed in all my documents to the official in the booth. I had no insurance for Morocco, and no green card for The Vespa either and the official threw the papers back at me,

"No insurance", he exclaimed.

Damn. What to do? I was told by my insurers that I would have to buy insurance at the border. After asking a few people at the border I was told that this was no longer possible.

What would I do?

## Bad man

Kev in the meantime, was at another kiosk doing the

same thing. He did have a green card and insurance and the official let him straight through.

Of course, I then rapidly went to the same kiosk as Kev, where I also got my papers stamped and went straight through. Unfortunately, the guy who helped Kev did not like me (as I filled out the forms myself and did not give him any money).

He called me a "Bad man".

This little "hustler" also knew I did not have any insurance as he watched me at the previous booth and threatened to tell the border officials this before I managed to enter Morocco.

"Ok. You win. How much do you want"? I said.

"10 Euros", was the reply.

I retaliated, "10 for that, you must be mad".

We settled on 5 Euros. I only had a 20 Euro note but he politely gave me 15 Euros change. I promptly got on my scooter and was about to ride off quickly. The alternative was to leave the scooter at the border with Kev, jump in a taxi with this little hustler, (I use the word 'hustler' lightly) and drive 35 km to get insurance for a premium price. No chance. I was not going to do that.

## Bud fan

Next, at the final checkpoint, the border official who was checking that all the papers were stamped correctly noticed something wrong with my documents.

Uh-oh! Has he realised I have no insurance?

And all the time Kev had been patiently waiting, literally just 10 metres away, sitting on Munchy, all set to go, just behind the official white line on the tarmac that signified the borderline between Europe and Africa. He was officially in Morocco. Meanwhile...

"Where did you get these papers stamped"? asked the border official.

I led him to the booth where I got the papers stamped, fearing the worst. Would I actually be allowed into Morocco after riding 2500km to get this far? Would I have to go to the nearest town in a taxi to Tetouan, to get insurance at an extortionate rate? Would we make it to the town of Chefchouean in time for supper? Would Kev's C90 go any further? All of these questions span through my mind as I stood helplessly, waiting for the verdict... I kept forcing a smile, hoping that would help somehow.

And all the time Kev had been patiently waiting, literally just 10 metres away, across the border.

# 10

## Morocco

Lovely Jubbly

I finally made it through the border and legged it for Chefchouean, in the Rif mountains of northern Morocco, which was about 100 km from the border. It was still early in the afternoon and I figured it would take us two hours to reach this little town in the hills.

After about 40 km we reached the town of Tetouan, the first major city from the border. We decided to stay there for the night. Actually, it was Kev's C90, Munchy the Crunchy, that dictated we should stop at the nearest place that would have a friendly mechanic as Munchy was not feeling too well.

As we approached Tetouan, and blindly looked for the entrance into the old Medina (old town) to find a hotel, a big, bald guy by the name of Abdul, a.k.a., Terry Tibbs Savalas, pulled up beside me on his big Honda motorbike and confessed to feeling "Lovely jubbly".

We exchanged hellos and I listened to more catchphrases from bygone TV shows mixed with a little cockney rhyming slang, all whilst trying to ride slow enough for Kev to catch up with us. I asked him if he knew of a cheap hotel.

"Follow me please. No worries mate".

## Hubbly Bubbly

Even though he would make a bit of commission from us, we followed Abdul straight to a cheap hotel (approx £6 per night for a room each) on the edge of the main square in the old Medina. That was a great result. Conveniently, there was a lock-up garage directly opposite the hotel that would be safe enough for us to leave our bikes in overnight (approx £1 per night). The rooms were basic but so was our transport so it suited us fine. We needed separate rooms because, although it would be more expensive, it meant that I could get a good night's sleep as Kev likes to snore loudly.

## Curly Wurly

Tetouan is a pleasant town. It has a European feel to it so it was an easy town to get to know and an easy introduction to Morocco. We never planned to stop here but as mentioned earlier, Munchy was not in good shape so we stopped earlier than planned. My Vespa was not in good shape either. It was not performing as well as before, although it did not seem as bad as Munchy.

Unfortunately, Kev had a few problems too. He was often found attached to an imaginary large, rubber band, the other end of which was connected to the hotel bathroom. As soon as he stepped foot outside the hotel, he quickly sprang back inside again. Or maybe he was practising his David Blaine vanishing act (which he also taught me but that comes a little later in the saga).

## Mr Whippy

After a good night's sleep and unpacking our bags

for the first time in what seemed like ages, Kev decided that the next morning Munchy needed an operation. After one night in the first hotel we fell into, I decided to look for an even cheaper hotel as we were going nowhere for a few days. The initial hotel was full of attractive distractions, namely giggling Berber girls hiding their smiles behind their headscarves. So we stayed at a different hotel, the Hotel Essalam which was even cheaper and a cleaner place too. It was also close enough to the place where we stored our bikes which meant we could easily check on them every now and then. I was worried my Vespa would get stolen. Not just here in Morocco but in Portugal and Spain too. So I always tried to find a place undercover and out of sight.

Dris, the guy at the hotel reception, was extremely helpful and friendly. Our Arabic was slowly getting better thanks to his patience and humour. We spent most nights outside, smoking and talking in a mix of French, Spanish, English and Arabic. None of which we were masters of.

The following days were spent searching for a surgeon/butcher for Munchy. I also needed some therapy, so I spent my time eating far too many French pastries and drinking copious amounts of strong, flavoursome fresh coffee. I was enjoying this life. Breakfast was often two fried eggs smothered in olive oil on top of the best bread I had ever tasted.

There was an art to eating it though as the only cutlery was a cocktail stick. The locals in the small cafe smoked their long pipes after every sip of coffee but I couldn't recognize the smell of any Kif or hash.

## Chocolate sprinkles

We were told by a few locals that there was a great mechanic with a fully equipped workshop in town - 'The biggest and the best'. We had searched all over town for this garage, walking for what seemed like miles, asking strangers if they knew the whereabouts of the big, one and only, motorcycle mechanic. After searching for two days we found him, almost at the bottom of the street where we were staying, just three or four minutes walk away from the hotel. All the maps that were drawn for us (one map had a series of straight lines and a picture of a bus on it), and all the directions we were given (this way for 3 or 4 km), were pretty useless. All the taxis we took, all the paths we walked on, in all the joints, in all the towns, in all the world, we eventually found this one. More by chance rather than by being pointed in the right direction. How we laughed!

# Pebble dash

Kev took his bike to the mechanic. The mechanic listened attentively to the running engine. He then laughed and gave an apology to Kev.

The mechanic then shouted to his colleagues to come and have a look at this weird bike.

They also laughed. More people came in to see what all the commotion was about, they looked, shook their heads, and murmured the Arabic equivalent of "Oh dear. No chance". When the chief mechanic then explained to everyone that this mad Englishman was going to ride this Honda to Marrakech everybody burst into tears. I was like the Biggus Diccus scene in The Holy Grail.

In local Arabic, the mechanic told Kev that, "If it was a camel I would shoot it, sell the carcass to the local tannery and with the profit, buy a small glass of coffee". At least that's what I imagined he said, as I don't speak any Arabic, especially the local dialect.

What actually happened was, Kev left the bike with the mechanic. After a couple of days, we returned to witness the engine in pieces on the workbench. The crankshaft had been removed. The problem lay there. The big end bearings on the crankshaft had decided to call it a day and retire from the spinning world of bearings and decided to knock instead of spin. Hence the loud engine noises Munchy was making.

We believe that new bearings were fitted but it was anybody's guess as the language barrier became as high as the price to fix it. That said, the mechanic worked extremely fast, putting aside all the other motorbikes in his garage to help Kev and Munchy get back on the road asap. Kev was extremely grateful to the mechanic and so with this joyous news we set off again the following day to our next destination, which was also the place I thought we may have reached on the first day, after leaving Portugal ten days ago.

## Hammered

We arrived in Chefchaouen after about two hours of riding. I arrived first, as usual, and proceeded with the customary, 'Wait-for-Kev routine', followed by the 'Get-bored-waiting-for-Kev' routine, then after 5 minutes finished with an 'I'll-have-to-meet-him-at-a-hotel-we-pre-agreed-to-meet-at-should-we-get-split-up-again' routine.

The reason I only waited for 5 minutes instead of 10 minutes was because the local big boys kept asking how much my scooter was worth.

Not, "Do you want to buy some hash"?

Or, "You want hotel"?

Or even, "Come to my shop and see some rugs".
But "How much is this [The Vespa] worth"?

This made me a little anxious since I have no insurance against theft. So naturally I legged it, or should I say, limped it, up the steep incline into the old Medina in search of the hotel that we planned to stay in.

Unfortunately for me, I had just done the kind of thing I told myself countless times not to do again... I asked a policeman for directions. He gave me directions but not necessarily the easiest or clearest of directions, sending me up another even steeper hill towards the small entrance gate to the old Medina. The Bab (gate/entrance) was barely big enough for my Vespa and I wasn't entirely sure I was allowed inside with my bike as it looked like a small narrow winding path with locals who were shopping and staring at me, wondering what I was about to try and do. Then a helpful guy lent me his son to show me the way to the hotel I enquired about, which I would never have found coming in from this direction.

## Spannered

What I was about to try and do was take the stupidest path into the heart of the old Medina I could imagine. Some paths were quite steep and all of them were very narrow, with some high steps that the scooter could not clear without being lifted. Aside from this, the place was also bustling, with old women, shopping for live chickens to kids playing in the narrow alleys. For The Vespa, which suffers from vertigo, it was all too much and it decided to stop going up any more hills. Luckily, the young kid I had borrowed, who was still sitting on the back of The Vespa, had lots of friends, who were all shouting his name as he rode past like a King on the passenger seat of The Vespa, and they then helped me push the scooter uphill, further into the old centre. I say 'helped'. They helped me push The Vespa, not necessarily in the right direction but they were all happy enough to give it their all and everyone enjoyed the spectacle.

I finally reached a downhill path without any steps and I 'bumped-started' The Vespa back into action and made it to the centre of town. I found the hotel we agreed to meet at and haggled my best but it was still too expensive. By this time, Kev came strolling towards me, thanked me for waiting for him and we then looked for another hotel with easier access for motorbikes. We found a most agreeable hotel with a most agreeable price and there we were, livin' la vida loca.

# You get the gist

I spent the next few days searching for some decent local produce, which proved to be harder than I imagined. There were plenty of guys offering the best of the best but it was the worst of the worst. But I eventually found something. Bhoom!

The next few days also consisted of me, on the hotel rooftop terrace, with my Vespa engine in pieces, replacing bearings and oil seals. I said I had a problem. Among other things, oil was leaking from the crankshaft onto my stator plate. I knew I did not do a very good job of changing the bearings and seals a few days before I left the UK so I packed some spares with me and have just finished putting everything back together. I searched for a workshop that could assist me with changing the bearings and also providing some sort of sealing paste. After a few sleepless nights, the engine was back in the chassis. It started on the second kick and ticked over pretty well for 30 seconds. I turned it off and that's how I left it as it was getting dark. I had carried all the tools I thought I would need to do a full engine strip and they all fitted in a small wash bag, stored neatly in the left side of the glove box behind the leg shields. It was a major risk, doing this kind of surgery on a hotel rooftop in a country that appeared to have no vespas, no spares or reliable mechanics. If it went wrong, if I lost another washer down in the crankcase again, for example, I would be up the creek without a paddle. I couldn't imagine pushing it all the way home so I had to make sure that I was confident in what I was doing and do it right the first time. It was all or nothing.

Looking back on this, I often wonder, deep in the back of my mind, why I took those spares and why I insisted on doing a full engine strip down on a hotel rooftop. I think I needed to prove something to myself. Prove that I had the skill and the knowledge and maybe even the stupidity to attempt such a thing. I had enough practice at home so I wasn't too phased by the thought, it wasn't much different apart from the fact that if I broke something I wouldn't be able to get any spares and I would very likely be stranded.

## No! You get the gist.

So the following day I went for a test drive with Kev, as he was also uncertain that his bike would make it to Fez, our next planned stopping point. Both bikes ran and performed well enough to continue the journey.

Trying to stay positive, I would say that we had not

actually broken down as such, in the sense that we were never stranded or needed assistance to get to a hotel but we did have a few teething problems. I think The Vespa didn't like the food in Morocco. It certainly wasn't used to mountain roads. The Vespa was resurrected in the flatlands of Norfolk, home of windmills, and so I guess felt a little intimidated by the mysterious Rif mountains.

Speaking of which, the food was fantastic. Kev found a place called 'Ali-Barbars' which made the best chicken and chips with salad baguettes ever. And they only cost the equivalent of £1. The rhythmic chopping and slicing and dicing of the chicken as it cooked on the large flat hot plate made for a memorable visit every time.

# 11

## Just like that

### North and South

It had been a long lie down which means we had become very lazy indeed and had not done much sightseeing. Our excuse was the weather. Whether or not we were going to get out of Chefchaouen. It was a nice enough place but after consistent rain for what seemed like 40 days and 40 nights, we decided enough was enough. Come rain or shine we will leave the next day. We waited for a small pocket of sunshine, put on all our wet weather gear, or a better description would be our wet, wet weather gear, and hit the road again. We headed south from the Rif mountains and planned to stop at the next city of Fez.

## Apples and Pears

We made an early start for the road to Fez (approx 200 km away) and I found out that 8 a.m. actually exists on my watch. Up to that point, I thought it only had 8 p.m.

The weather wasn't ideal but it was ok. We started with all of our wet, wet weather gear on, found the pocket of sunshine and got out of town fast. Well, as fast as the cylinder bore would allow.

I would like to say it was all downhill but alas, no. We still climbed our way up through the mountain roads. The bikes made progress though. The surgery I performed on The Vespa, on the rooftop, seems to have paid off. It sounded very different but I was not so sure if that was a good thing or a bad thing. It sounded like it would go faster, so I remained positive and decided it could only be a good thing.

Munchy the Crunchy (by the way - I found out - she's a girl) was running kind of ok too. Not great but not exceptionally bad. We had plenty of time to let that happen.

We also found out on the way that dogs like to try

and eat my side panels but only when I was riding at 100 km/h past the gate/driveway they were guarding.

Munchy the Crunchy makes donkeys re-enact the mad MB game 'Buckaroo'.

Riding the same speed as Kev made me want to go to sleep but I think it must have been part of the David Blaine act that he performed.

But more importantly, we found out that the mechanic in Tetouean was a better magician than Kev and performed various cunning stunts on his engine such as the, 'Now-you-hear-the-banging now-you-don't, now-you-hear-the-banging-again-but-its-louder' routine.

Amazing.

## Mine's a pony, raise you a monkey

On the way to Fez, whilst we stopped to adjust some loose nuts, we were passed by a few old Peugeot 205s and old Land Rovers with English registration plates, all dressed with rally stickers, roof racks, spare tyres and spotlights. That's what we needed on our machines! Big rally stickers with large numbers on, maybe that would make us more reliable and maybe even help us to go faster. They were all

1991, 'J' reg' models and from the U.K.

We quickly packed our screwdrivers away and chased after them, like it was a challenge to catch them on the mountain roads. I wanted to know what they were doing. Where were they going? After several km, we just about managed to catch up with them and Kev was menacingly close.

He took the lead and... wait for it ladies and gentlemen... he overtook a car. Yes, it was true, you read it here first.

OK, so it was only an old Peugeot 205 but something more amazing than that happened.

He overtook the Land Rover too. I was watching from the rear of the convoy of 205s and Land Rovers with glee.

"Look at Munchy go", I cried.

The looks on the faces of those guys and girls driving their old bangers through Morocco must have been of total amazement. Somehow it was really funny. Seeing even more old bangers riding passed them. It gave that particular day some kind of meaning. Some connection to something we left behind. It would have made a great aerial shot from a drone, had they been available back then. Those fellow adventurers were being overtaken by little old Munchy the Crunchy. A Honda C90. A top of which was a determined Kev. The road began to straighten up so Kev went for the 'Right-I'm-going-to-have-the-lot-of-you' manoeuvre and proceeded to overtake the remaining two rally vehicles in one class move. What style!

Munchy was happy munching away the km and those rally drivers were left flabbergasted I was sure and left still wondering what happened to us. I watched from behind and laughed out loud at this moment in sheer admiration for Kevin and Munchy. They had just been overtaken by a C90.

I waited for the rally drivers to recompose themselves and then surprised them by whizzing past them all. One or two of the drivers/passengers waved back but most seemed to want to ignore the fact that they had just been overtaken again but this time by an old Vespa.

We watched them go past us again later when we stopped for coffee but I think they didn't see us as we sheltered from the sudden downpour of rain in a cafe. Hello, darkness my old friend.

## Major

It was a nice scenic route that took us straight to Fez before 6 pm. Once again whilst riding around the outside of the old Medina walls looking for the right entrance, I took a stupid route and this time it took us through the fruit and veg market. Much to the dismay of the locals. But I knew my hotel was just inside this gate. But as we approached the Bab/the gate, there was one major difference.

There was no vanishing act, no waiting or wondering where he was. Kev was directly behind me and he followed me in! We made it to the same town at the same time. I believe it was the force of Tommy Cooper.

After quickly haggling down the price of a hotel room and parking our bikes in another underground car park, we were in another hotel in another town.

## Miner

Our first impressions of Fez were not so good. A drunk made us feel welcome by deliberately barging into us when we were carrying our bags to the hotel. Well, he more or less bounced off Kev and took revenge on me by attempting to kick me. I was not in the mood for a fight and ignored him. The hotel we ended up staying in was not too good. Kev had a makeshift 'en-suite sunken bath' in his room. It was still raining, inside and out, the food was more expensive than we were used to, the hotel was rubbish and the welcoming committee was rather rude, to say the least.

"I'm leaving at 7 a.m. and getting out of here", were

Kev's first comments.

I remained quiet as the weather did not look like it was going to get any better. Earlier, in Chefchouean, people had warned us that there would be extremely bad weather coming the following morning. As bad as the experience was, I was prepared to stay another day in Fez and sit out the storm that everybody had forecast and explore the old town.

## Baker

At early o'clock the next morning a bang on the door from Kev woke me up.

"Come on then, let's go", he said with a deep sigh.

My reply was a little less friendly. I was ready to change hotels but did not want to be riding in what looked like another storm that was approaching. I tried to talk him out of it but he was having none of it. He was leaving. Whatever happened? So I thought I had better keep with him and kind of reluctantly tagged along.

We rode in what was probably the worst weather I had ever ridden in during the whole trip so far and I was riding in it against my better judgement which did not put me in a great mood. After 2 hours of battling with the rain and the wind, I almost stopped at one of the few houses I saw dotted along the long, open, straight, uphill highway to ask for a bed for the night. I had almost had enough. In all my years of riding, I had never felt this way before no matter how bad the weather was. I had ridden in worse rain than this, but not for this length of time. It was just relentless. The road was straight, long and boring. When I stopped for a quick break in an abandoned shelter I checked the tiny map I had and looked for the next town or hotel. The map said to 'keep straight for 315 km'.

"Interesting", I thought. I was asking myself, "Why am I riding in this crappy weather"? I knew the answer which wound me up even more. The answer lay way behind me somewhere on a C90. He too was beginning to ask himself the same question.

## Whaler

I stopped at the first hotel I saw. I entered, dripping wet and shrugged my shoulders towards the two policemen drinking coffee, who had the expression of, "Yep. It's raining alright".

I asked the price of a room at the reception, scooped my jaw from the floor, shrugged again and got ready to be beaten up by the weather once more. I didn't realise hotels could be quite so expensive.

The directions out of town were not so clear (never ask a foreign policeman for directions, I kept forgetting that) and I ended up heading in the wrong direction. After 15 minutes the force turned me back the way I came, back into the town of Ifrane. There was no doubt about it. It will definitely rain. Snow too. Yes, Snow! Something I really wasn't expecting on my way to Marrakesh. While I was there, standing at the crossroads, getting soaked through to the skin, and deciding which path I should take, I bumped into Kev who had the same problem as I had. It was only about another 15km to the next town which had cheaper hotels but we did not even make it that far. After 2 or 3 km the weather defeated us and we stopped at a motel and asked for a room. This hotel was much more reasonable, about £30 a night (we were used to paying around £5 a night) and Kev, to his credit, offered to pay, due to the fact that;

a) it was Xmas

b) he was such an idiot for making us ride in the worst weather we had had so far on that trip.

But, with Kev's generosity and after we had the chance to dry our clothes in a nice warm hotel (the stairs and the bathrooms were heated - luxury!) it made us more cheerful and we left the next day feeling more refreshed and ready to go.

# Bob Marley

No Bob Marley.

# 12

# Christmas

## Swiss

In the morning, after a great night's sleep for me in a large double bed and for Kev, on the heated bathroom floor, we were ready for another day. Thankfully, when we woke up in the morning, inside the nice warm Swiss-style Ifrane hotel, in a pleasant Swiss-style town that had pointy red roofs and lots of snow, we found that the weather was sunny at last. We also found out that this hotel was 1650 metres above sea level and has fine skiing in the area. We also found out that Ifrane (no it's not a made-up name and there should be no ifs or buts about it, it does rain) has the most snow in Morocco. That probably explains the reason why our bikes struggled so much. We did not notice how steep the roads were as our heads were down, trying to hang on for dear life in the torrential wind and rain we rode through.

## Tony

Christmas day. Khenifra, just 100km away, was our next destination. Long gone are the days in Europe when we used to say, " Come on, let's go 300 km to the next country".

It had been slow going. I even stopped a couple of times to adjust my timing as The Vespa seemed so slow. Very slow. It didn't help though.

Passing through the little villages and towns there was a police checkpoint which, as I had no insurance, I didn't stop... I just carried on, made eye contact and waved at the policeman as I slowly went past him. He was too confused to stop me... Did he just see a smiling Englishman riding a Vespa through his town? Yes, he did. Kev stopped but he wasn't sure what the policeman wanted and so followed my lead and carried on again. We noticed that half the houses were being propped up with scaffold poles due to the same extremely, ferociously bad weather that we had suffered the previous day. Sandbags and boats were issued to all concerned. It was that bad. Noah would have loved it here.

We found some food in town. Food. Now there's a subject me and Kev spend endless hours talking about and applauding. The food has been quite nice. Maybe not as spicy as I had imagined. A different style to what I was used to but overall, very tasty.

## Family Robinson

   Khenifra was home to a university which meant lots of students. As we went out in search of food we caused a small ripple of admiration from some of the locals. Even when they are out with their mothers the girls could not help but smile shyly at the English talent. Unfortunately, we never made it to the local Disco we were invited to. Kev got so excited at the thought that he snapped his kickstart in half, which he later got welded back together in town. It was here in Khenifra that he found out that he could get a brand-new engine for Munchy. 110cc or 125cc. What a choice. The choice was actually, what does he want....? Chinese or Japanese? I don't think this was the first time he's had this choice either but that's another story.

## The Waltons

After a couple of days, celebrating Christmas by unwrapping a small bottle of wine I carried with me (it was a gift from my sister) we got back on our bikes, which had begun to squeak and knock more than ever. It sounded like my bearings needed changing once more and Munchy needed some serious attention. The Vespa was drinking about 3 x more petrol than usual so frequent stops were needed.

At one petrol station, we stopped for a coffee. After a leisurely drink I went to pay, using my finest local dialect I thought I had picked up.
"Kawha, bisshal?", I coughed. Which as far as I was aware meant - 'How much for the coffee'?
"9 Dirham" was the snappy reply.

I smiled back at him and said, "Bezzaf"! in an astonished tone. Meaning - 'That's a lot'! - It wasn't actually expensive. I was just trying some friendly banter.

The waiter leaned forward onto his toes and over the counter and staring straight into my face asked, "Problem"? in a rather menacing way.

"No problemo". Meaning - 'I'll get my coat'.

Lesson learnt.

As I walked out of the cafe I whispered to Kev along with a signal that suggested we get out of there sharpish but he was too busy making himself comfortable as he watched a local farmer direct the traffic, which consisted of just 2 cars, a tractor and 5 cats.

"Kev! Psssst"!

"Huh? What"?

"Let's get out of here, it's going to kick off".

Two things I found out in life later that day were;

1) Vespas and C90s are not really made for fast getaways in sticky situations.

2) Kev still wasn't sure what had just happened. Neither was I really but I thought it best just to leave quickly. I didn't mean to offend anyone.

Our escape was like watching 2 snails trying to get out of the soup bowl they found themselves in as we slowly and casually got ready to ride again.

Nothing bad happened. There was nothing to see there. We went on our merry way once more into the Tit n' Ziza region towards Beni-Mellal Marrakech. In true spirit, we arrived in town at different times of the day. Without realising I had passed Kev whilst he was filling up with petrol, I carried on through Beni-Mellal towards Marrakech.

## What am I now, What am I now?

We had set our rendezvous point to Beni-Mellal which was about 260 km from Marrakech. I could almost smell it, it was so close. I considered going straight there. But, as I headed out of town the force sent me back again and it was there where I ended up staying the night. I wasn't sure where David Blaine had got to this time but I was sure he was safe and enjoying himself.

In my hotel there were a couple of Italians staying, one of which said he had to have a peep under the poncho I used as a bike cover, to see if it was what he thought it was. And it was what he thought it was. A Vespa. He admired it so much. In fact, more than the big rental bike with heated grips he used for his adventure that was parked next to The Vespa and he admitted a little envy for not choosing a Vespa for himself.

## Little House on the Prairie

I awoke early the next morning to somehow catch Kev waiting for me in a large petrol station out of town. David Blaine rides again. I refilled the 8-litre petrol tank and suggested we catch up over coffee in the first place we came across.

I later found out that Kev headed into Beni-Mellal. Probably as I was heading out of town. The force sent me back into town, whilst Kev's force sent him back out of town. So we were forced in and out of town like magnets. Our paths never crossed.

# Kwai Chang Caine

Pleased with a good day's riding on a nice, sunny day, Kev had decided to venture on towards our goal - Marrakesh. He made great progress too and went for a further 100km on his own. But in his haste and as his C90 was going faster than the speed of light, he accidentally ran over an old lady. He did not see her as the lights on Munchy were a little dim, to say the least. Also, riding into the dazzling, setting sun did not help matters either. He said that the old lady spun around on her heels, clutching her washing basket like the housekeeper in the Tom and Jerry cartoons and wondered what the hell had just happened to her. Kev did not hang around to find out. He ended up reflecting on the day in a nice hotel. No, not a Moroccan jail cell but a proper nice hotel with a swimming pool, jacuzzi and where a massage was only 5 Dirham. Allegedly.

Marrakesh was now in our sights. We followed in the direction of the Atlas mountains.

Since arriving in Morocco it had taken us about 23 days to get this far. A few more hours and we honestly believed we were going to be in Marrakesh, in time for tea, fairy cakes and a nice slice of Waterhog flan.

We made it and for the second time only on this trip, we arrived at our destination, on the same road, at the same time, on the same day. Amazing!

We headed for a great, cheap hotel that I had stayed at before. Although it was full, we were able to 'book a mattress' on the rooftop terrace. We had some more food (another tagine) and had a quick shower and had a walkabout.

I noticed Kev started to shake and foam at the mouth.

"What's wrong"? I asked.

He turned south and silently pointed with a big smile with eyes glazed.

"Alcohol", he said surprisingly, "I smell alcohol".

## Grasshopper

After 7 weeks with no booze, Kev, who now took on the stance of a bloodhound chasing an escaped criminal, eagerly set off towards the Grand Hotel Tazi, with me chasing after him as fast as I could.

"I must have some booze. I demand to have some booze", I could almost hear Kev shout.

The bar was about to close. We had to work fast, "A pair of quadruple whiskies and another pair of pints please landlord"............

So we made it to our ultimate destination on our little shopping bikes. That deserved a drink. In the bar, we met someone else who told us we were mad. Thanks, Ian! In the past, he had owned Vespas and C90s and had been to Marrakech about 30 years before. We enjoyed a few beers and shared some old stories.

We met most people in the bar of the Grand Hotel or on the rooftop terrace of the Hotel Ali, which I can highly recommend if you need somewhere cheap to stay in Marrakech. Ask for room 101.

Ali, the manager, spent a lot of time haggling with me for The Vespa. Of course, I would never sell it. Not even for the 200 Euros he was offering. Now I know how the vineyard owner in Portugal felt.

If you want to know anything about 'all you can eat' buffets at the Hotel Ali then Martin is the man. He was another comrade staying at the Ali and he couldn't get enough of those buffets. (That's buffettes to all that know him). Although he betrayed the buffets after a couple of weeks and turned to Pizzas for company.

## Hitch Hike

Then there was Oliver from Belgium. We met him on the rooftop too and he told us he had hitchhiked all the way here. I would do the same if I lived in Belgium. Oliver did not have the same time scale as me and Kev and he ended up going to meet his folks at the airport two days in advance. We use the traditional way of telling which day it is, or how long ago something happened, by how many moons had passed. Or for a longer time scale, how many shaves we had had. Or for an even longer period of time, how many haircuts we had had. We could also define the date by working out how many mechanics we had used. This brings us neatly to the continuing saga of 'Munchy the Crunchy'.

## The Monkey

After leaving Tetouan all those shaves and a haircut ago, Munchy was still feeling poorly. She was still knocking and banging on the way to Marrakech. In Marrakech Kev found another mechanic to carry out more open heart surgery on poor Munchy.

Now, most of the mechanics workshops we have witnessed, although small, appeared to be well equipped. Although I suspect that all the spanners, sockets, pliers etc hanging neatly on the wall were there just to keep the nails that were supporting them from falling out. So they were left well alone. The tools that were used were as follows;

1 x screwdriver and 1 x small hammer.

Now if these two tools could not do the job then a larger hammer was called for. The young lad ran in and out of the workshop, trying various size hammers to hit the end of the screwdriver with. These hammers were far too big to be hung up and were readily available on the floor, where all the work was carried out. Being close at hand, the hammers were in frequent use. Imagine Mike Oldfield playing Tubular Bells on a morning of hammers on a workshop floor.

## The Peanut Duck

To be fair, the chief mechanic, who worked on Munchy was pretty thorough and sneakily used a few specialist tools such as spanners and sockets but only when he thought no one was looking.

Kev had turned into his alter ego, David Blaine again and had disappeared, I couldn't be too sure exactly what work was carried out on the engine, as I was too busy waiting for my parts to arrive - I decided to order so spares from Beedspeed, U.K. who were very helpful although quite surprised when I told them where I was and where I wanted the parts shipped to.

They seemed quite pleased as posting to Morocco was a first for them.

Getting back to the C90. I believe that another new crank and new bearings were fitted. Along with new valves. I also believed that the parts used were probably made for the similar kind of bikes that were found all over Morocco, namely the Yamaha Mate or the Chinese equivalent, the Docker C90. They look the same at least!

We worked out that the previous mechanic must have changed the original Honda crank for a knackered Chinese one, which turned out to be just as bad, probably worse.

I was at the mechanic's workshop to witness the all-new Munchy being tested out by the mechanic after he had finished working on it. He was popping wheelies up and down the street like a true pro. Why was the wheelie the only way to test a rebuilt engine I wondered.

It seemed like Munchy was a new woman! This almost leads us neatly to the continuing saga of, 'What I did on my winter vacation'.

# 13

## New Year's Eve

January 2010

Sniff

It was New Year's Eve, my friends. And it would not be the last. The bar of
 The Grand Hotel was pretty full. We celebrated in traditional style, drinking. We made friends with other globe-trotters and were grateful for the late-night drink after midnight. Sat next to us were a couple of globe-trotters from Texas and Australia. We got chatting and decided to try and find another bar in the more up-market part of town. After a long walk, we found a few potential bars. After we asked about the admission

price to these upmarket joints, we decided that the Grand Hotel was not a bad place to bring in the new year after all. Hootenanny!

The drunken Spanish and Argentinians we tried to make sense of were in high spirits. The 'Toilet clerk' was also in very high spirits. He was the guy who insisted that everyone should leave a tip for him on a plate placed just outside the toilets. (Don't eat yellow snow springs to mind) If you did not leave a tip, he cursed you to die in Hell whilst he pissed on the floor, swallowing another lung full of the glue he was potentially sniffing.

## Superglue

We had a new compadre who came to join us for a few days.

One shave later, when all the New Year's sparklers had fizzled out, we went to meet our friend Sue at Marrakech airport. Unfortunately, the weather was foggy and the plane had been diverted to Agadir, a four-hour bus journey southwest of Marrakech. So four hours later, in the afternoon, we went again to the airport. This time we found her ready and waiting for us.

My 'one-thing-a-day' routine would now involve at least two things a day. How would I cope with this busy schedule? Actually I coped pretty well. Sue was great company and was a welcome change for Kev and me, what with having to put up with each other for so long. After we all arrived at the Souk el-Attarine I booked her a room in the Ali. We then showed her the way to the nearest bar and she was never seen again. Only kidding.

We ended up booking a tour together, going by minibus to the desert of Zagora. Apologies go to The Vespa and Munchy for not taking them there. They were tired and needed a rest. It would have been a long and arduous journey for both machines straight through the Atlas mountains. Especially as they were feeling so poorly at the time.

For us to book the tour to the desert we had to sell Sue to the tour operator. He did, after all, offer the princely sum of 2,000 camels. On condition that Sue joined the Jedi clan and bought a black Jedi outfit. An offer we could not refuse. In between booking the trip, drinking tea and selling our mate for 2,000 camels, we noticed that the weather was getting a little fierce. Would the rain that followed us all the way here follow us to the desert too? Kev is adamant that I was cursed by prevailing bad weather. We shall find out the next day. We had an early start the next morning, and I mean, really early. So early in fact that I still don't know what time we left.

# Pritt Stick

On the bus with us were couples from France, Spain and Brazil. (Hi, to Patricia and Miguel from Brazil). I confess to finding all that out on the return journey as I was in the Twilight Zone on the way there. The scenery was spectacular. I wished The Vespa had seen these mountain roads.

The all-inclusive 2-day tour to the desert, everything included except drinking water and lunch. Well, almost everything was included. Except for breakfast on the first morning. Lunch at an overpriced restaurant. The evening meal was a tagine shared between six people but that was included. The breakfast in the morning barely broke my fast (included) and again the not included lunch at an overly priced restaurant, followed by the not included teas and coffees en route (more French) and the not included evening meal on the second day. Also, the long turban head scarves that the tout said we needed to protect us from the sand and the wind and the desert sun... we're not included. God forbid, I almost had to get my wallet out.

Thankfully, Superglue had bought 2 scarves with her, one of which I borrowed. As for Kev, he had his crash helmet with him so he was fully protected!

# Camel Toe

We found that Dromedary Camels were very uncomfortable to ride. At least, not as comfortable as The Vespa. Kev ended up with a massive scar on his buttock cheeks because the seat was so uncomfortable.

I had difficulty resting my bags comfortably whilst on the dromedary and ended up riding side saddle to the Berber tents, just visible in the distant sand dunes.

After we arrived at camp, we listened to exotic tales of Berber life around a campfire. Ancient, mystical stories of a nomadic tribe who had to survive on their instincts and navigate by the stars, were told with great admiration, only to be cut short by a Britney Spears ringtone coming from the pocket of the chief storyteller.

"...Oh yeh, can you record Eastenders for me"? he may have said.

# Through the eye of a needle

Kev missed this epic story as he had disappeared once more into the stunningly beautiful and organic sand dunes of the Sahara desert to look in awe at the stars while he took a dump.

The stars....! Wow! The stars in the evening desert! What a beautiful site. Truly. Amazing. In a clear sky with no pollution, there appeared to be many more stars than I had ever witnessed anywhere in the world. I left Kev to count how many new stars he could see, whilst I mansplained to Superglue the obligatory introduction to the stars.

"That's the Milky Way that is", was about as far as I got before Superglue passed Kevin 5 Dirhams (about £0.50p) to pay for the bet they had arranged earlier - How long would it take before someone pointed out the bleedin' obvious.


After a very memorable experience in the desert, we headed back towards Marrakech to claim the 2,000 camels that we were promised.

The Tagines, couscous and coffee were also calling me closer to the cafes and Kev closer to the toilets.

# 14

## What really happened

### Disappear

Yeh? Hang on a minute! What really happened?

I couldn´t remember much. I´d started growing a beard and my system of measuring time (1 x shave = 3 or 4 days) had grown out of the window. I wrote stupid cartoon scripts in a euphoric haze on a cloud of smoke.

Kev had been practising his dark magic, ready for his finale. Which reminded me that my French was improving.

His final disappearing trick was to leave Marrakech and Morocco and reappear on a totally different continent altogether. Now, that's magic.

I still believe to this day that Kev sold Munchy to a hareem. She always did turn a few heads when she was coming down the street. People even walked into lamp posts they didn't realise were there, as they concentrated on watching Munchy roar past.

## Or, for our friends in Norwich - Despair

The crux of the matter was that Munchy munched her way through Kev's wallet faster than anticipated and Kev had to file for a divorce from Munchy. She was a high-maintenance, low-speed kind of crunchy and Kev just could not keep up with her demands any longer.

So alas, it is so, that, there came a day, when, lo, it came to be, that, Kev, had to leave poor Munchy laying lonely in a hotel basement. For tax reasons, he never actually sold Munchy but instead, pawned her.

We are all hoping that Munchy would still be there when we will one day return to Marrakech. Flying there would definitely be the cheapest option to do that, as opposed to riding a moped there via Portugal.

A very helpful guy in the Ali offered to help Kev out and made him an offer he could refuse.

But Kev did not refuse the deal and went ahead,

sold Munchy and booked a flight to Seville, Spain, where he would then somehow get to Portugal, where his van and his sanity were waiting for him.

## Diss

And so it was, Munchy the Crunchy was left behind in Marrakech. Kev had to sell her to pay for a flight back to Portugal. Unfortunately, he could only get an expensive flight to nearby Sevilla, Spain. So when he reached Spain he would then probably have to sell his shoes to pay for the bus ticket he needed to get to Portugal.

Once in Portugal, he would then need to sell his boat to get the money to take his van to Marrakech, where he would have to sell his van to get the money for riding Munchy back to Portugal. When he reached Portugal he would then have to sell Munchy again to pay for a flight to the U.K. so he could get a job to pay for the return trip to Portugal to buy poor Munchy back. Then go back to Moroc......

You get the idea by now.......

## Pair

But hey!
It was all irrelevant.

There was good news.

I later heard from Kev that Munchy had given birth to Munchy II.

And Munchy II will soon be old enough to join Munchy in Morocco very soon.

Probably next summer. Maybe.

So this left me and The Vespa in Marrakech, all alone, wondering what to do next. I still had to ride it home after all, which meant I was only halfway through my trip. I was still under the 'get-me-home repair', which I very much hoped would get me home.

Do I wait for those elusive spares to turn up or do I head for Spain where I would be able to replace the bearings?

Do I head south as per my earlier plans?

Who knew?

## Coconuts

I decided that I could not live the dream forever and so reluctantly decided to leave Marrakesh. It was getting too expensive to stay amongst the distractions of city life.

# 15

## On the road again

Canned Heat

Leaving Marrakech behind, I took the old road towards Casablanca, avoiding the toll road. To avoid it I had to turn around on the deserted dual carriageway that led directly to the toll booths which were in direct sight, going the wrong way down the dual carriageway, then found the old road.
Aside from the fact that I was careful with my money (I'm sure Kev would agree), the main reason for not taking the fast toll road was the lack of petrol stations along the way. I didn't fancy running out of petrol on a

toll road. It would also be boring. There would be no dogs chasing me there.

## Woodstock

On the old road, I was frantically flagged down by a couple of guys on their makeshift Chinese 3-wheeler tractor. I thought The Vespa was on fire or something by the way they were frantically signalling me to stop. It turned out that they had run out of fuel. I gave one of the guys a lift to the nearest petrol station further up the road. It wasn't the first time I stopped to pick up a hitchhiker. So far I had picked up an old lady with her shopping, a school kid who just got off the bus and a farmer who was late for his dinner. Now it was somebody else's turn.

I was aiming for the town of Kenitra, some 350 km from Marrakech. But I missed the turning I needed to avoid going straight into Casablanca. Casablanca was by far the biggest city in Morocco that I had been to. And it was a long way in. So into Casablanca, I went. Choking on the fumes as I got closer to the centre.

Stopping for petrol I ended up adding a small bottle of 2-stroke oil into my petrol tank, as usual. Only this time I spilt some on my fingers and panicked when I realised it was not oil I had just poured into my petrol but an engine oil additive to stop leaks in car engines, which I had bought earlier in Chefchaoueuan. Unfortunately, I used an empty bottle of 2-stroke oil to store it in and got confused and poured it into my freshly filled fuel tank.

"Damn" and "Blast" were two words I did not use but for the sake of our younger readers, they will suffice. It took me over an hour to drain the full 8-litre tank by unscrewing the fuel pipe from the carb and draining the tank into some discarded plastic water bottles that were laying around. I then refilled with fresh petrol and made sure I added 2-stroke oil this time and set off once more towards the capital, Rabat.

## Jimi Hendrix

The old road to Rabat was blocked off and the fuzz told me to take the toll road, which I did. I was passed by the usual people who seemed to like The Vespa, honking and waving and giving me the thumbs up (Thumbers). I don´t know if it was because they liked Vespas or if they were surprised to see one screaming past them at 100 km/h on a toll road. At the end of the road I paid the toll at the booth, where the guy asked me,

"Didn't you get stopped by the fuzz (police)"?

"No", was my puzzled reply. "Why do you ask"?

"That's a moped that is and that's not allowed on big boys' roads".

Cheeky. My little Vespa was a 200cc scooter, not a C90!

Moped? Phaah! Kinnigits! And rode off laughing.

# Foxy Lady

I finally reached Kenitra at about 6 pm and it was dark. The first thing I noticed was the number of bars and nightclubs around town. That probably explained all the drunks I had to avoid who were wandering in and around the paths and roads with less abandonment than a freely wandering sacred cow.

I checked into the first hotel I found, which turned out to be an expensive 3-star hotel with its own bar and discotheque. Excellent. Maybe now I can teach everybody how to do the Peanut Duck. Not.

At the crowded bar, Katrina from Kenitra decided she wanted to take me home with her. Guessing her circumstances I declined the offer. I paid a lot of money to stay in that hotel and by gosh I was going to sleep there! Although she was a nice enough lady, she just wasn't my type, what with her being old enough to have built the Medina and trying her best to get me to buy her drinks. After, she went off in a 'huff' because I refused to buy her drinks and I ended up talking to a couple of locals who liked to get drunk. One of them, surprisingly, liked to drink pints.

All I can say to these guys is, "Oued Sabou daze naid".

To which Mohammad's reply would be, "Touts naid floors".

Don´t ask me what it means. I was too busy rolling on the floor holding my stomach, laughing hard.

He told me he was talking in English. I didn't believe a word of it.

What I did believe however was that these Moroccan guys hated the

French even more than we Brits do.

"Yeh... How much"?

After a short and thoughtful pause came their reply," ...a lot".

I had to decline the offer of staying at Mounir's bachelor pad the next day as I needed to get back to Blighty sooner rather than later. Thanks, Mounir. We will eat at Mohammad's restaurant next time. Get the beers in. Wadsboozedazenaide.

## The Lady of the Lake

The next day, feeling a little hazy, I headed out of

town towards a large nature reserve which I had hoped would be crowded with flocks of Flamingos and migrating birds who stop there, along with herds of Wildebeest roaming majestically through the plains and migratory European swallows gripping coconuts by the husk. But alas no. There wasn't that much to see on this occasion. A few ducks, that was about it. At this point, I remembered my home town of Diss with its ducks and mere - a small, deep lake.

Now I was alone, I had more opportunities to stop to take some photos, mainly of The Vespa, who was now getting used to the camera and started posing without a care in the world.

I was by the fishing port of Kenitra when I suddenly realised that I was missing my phone. I likely left it on the seat while I put on my helmet and shades and forgot about it. I think it may have fallen on the road somewhere near the traffic-calming hump in the road that I didn't notice until it was too late. I also didn't realise that The Vespa knew how to fly. Just how high was that last speed bump?

So, I believe that some lucky fisherman had a great catch that day and was the proud owner of a Nokia brick. I rode around looking for it, asking around in some nearby shops but to no avail. I had barely used it and it could be replaced. I was a little disheartened but carried on as normal. I only used it now and again to get an overview of a small map. I would have been more upset if I had lost my camera. Not because it was expensive but because of all the photos I had on it. I like to travel light, so I carefully chose what I considered to be the smallest, cheapest and the best at the time, which was a Ricoh R8.

A little later, whilst posing for the camera, The Vespa lost its footing in the sand and fell over a couple of times. It may have been drunk with excitement, getting so much attention from the camera. Maybe it was the
 side effects of the engine additive I added the day before by mistake that made it dizzy. I drove around and found a cheap hotel room with TV - what a bonus. All for 70Dh. (£0.50p).

# 16

# A Morning of Hammers

## Up North

Leaving my phone behind, I headed north once more. This time, I was heading towards Tetouan, the first town Kev and I stopped at when we first arrived in Morocco. That also meant that I was nearing the end of my Moroccan adventure, something I was not looking forward to. So I decided to stop off at a town called Larache on the way, where I stayed for a couple of nights, trying to prolong the inevitable.

The only trouble I had was in my hotel room, where I had to watch the same TV channel the receptionist was watching downstairs. It was late and after fighting a losing battle with the remote, I decided that Miss Marples in Arabic with French subtitles was not all that bad.

Then, at the critical moment in the gripping crime thriller, the channel promptly changed to an important debate between Moroccan dignitaries. After 10 minutes, I discovered how to change channels but unfortunately, Miss Marples was the best the TV could offer. Then the downstairs receptionist changed channels again. This time it stuck to Portuguese football.

Moroccans love football. Every night, in all the bars, in all the towns, in all of Morocco, I imagined football was watched by the thousands. The coffee bars were always full of spectators, spectating football. During all the small conversations I had with locals, all about football, I had to fake an interest in the sport. I am British, English and as such many people abroad expected me to love 'the football'. I told them that Chelsea was my team. It was the first team that sprang to mind. They babbled back with a mixture of consonants, syllables and some big clusters of the two, which I guessed were all names of football players. I recognized a few names but I could not repeat them. I was a little out of my depth. I could not tell you who Chelsea had just signed or who won the cup. The only cups in these coffee bars were the ones used to drink tea and I noticed that men here drank tea like it was whisky and they drank whisky like it was tea. Many of them also smoked like a 36-year-old 2-stroke Vespa.

# Down South

So there I was, at 10 pm, still in my Larache hotel room, watching Portuguese footballers falling over on TV.

In the room above me, I could hear the occupants rising from their beds, ready to start their night shift of moving furniture. Moving furniture around their room. They must have bad Feng Shui because they could not decide where to permanently position everything.

In the room below, was an extremely rowdy board game going on. Checkers, most likely. Or some other board game that involved incessant banging and shouting.

In the room next door was a carpenter, practising for his master's degree in hammering nails into hardwood. He still needed a lot of practice by the sound of things.

Next, the noise outside my door, which sounded like a heavy lady beating the living daylights out of a large rug with a huge cast-iron spade, was in fact, a large lady beating the living daylights out of a heavy rug with a massive cast-iron shovel.

The following morning when I woke up to a morning of hammers, I sat and decided that enough was enough. The surround sound of night shifters made me want to shift so I decided I had better start the 100km journey back to... Tetouan. I had to start thinking about heading back home due to lack of money. I had some offers of work that I could not refuse. Oh no! W*rk. What a ridiculous word that seemed to be. Back to bed, back to reality. Later, I headed for Tetouan.

# 17

## Meanwhile

### Flight

Although Kev was no longer with me for the return journey, he still gave me plenty to write about. Even without Munchy he still had a story to tell.

After he betrayed his beloved Munchy and sold her to a hareem to pay for a flight to Spain, Kev arrived at Sevilla airport. Once there he had to wait 12 hours for a bus to take him to Portugal. During that 12 hours, with very little money, he walked around a bit, taking in the sights of the lovely city. As a result of this, his feet began to blister. So he found a nice quiet spot to sit and chill. Whilst he waited for the bus. He was approached by two of the fuzz.

"Passport", they demanded.

# Fight

Kev obliged and they seemed happy enough that he was not the kind of suspected criminal that he resembled. Later, two more people, claiming to be the fuzz, approached Kev with the same demand. He nervously handed one of them his passport, only after he had seen their I.D. badge and had also noticed the gun the guy was discreetly showing him, hidden under his jacket.

The passport was then passed onto another guy, who started to walk off with it. Kev's alarm bells started to ring loudly and in the same manner that he demanded beer wherever he went, he demanded that they return his passport. Sharpish!

Which they did.

Rather promptly.

# Photo Fit

During that day, more of the fuzz asked Kev for his I.D. It must have been the nice jumper which he bought in Chefchouan that made him look like a homeless guy, which in turn made him stand out from the crowd.

He finally caught his bus to Portugal and ended up

in Tavira, close to his final destination. There were no taxis around at that time of the night, not that he had enough money for a taxi anyway. He picked up his bag, gritted his teeth and walked the remaining 4 km or 5km with blistered feet.

He eventually reached the villa in complete darkness. It was the same villa we had stayed at earlier. It was not easy to get in. The gate had to be dismantled. He had to find his key. He found that there was lots of mud around. Or at least he had hoped it was just mud. He could not quite see. All he heard was the squelching of his mud-filled boots and the chorus of frogs in the background.

# 2 Bob Bits

His dodgy stomach never quite made it all the way home without mishap either. At least he eventually made it back to the villa in one piece. After 21 hours of travelling, he finally fell asleep in a tired slumber.

The next few days, whilst he waited for me to stop messing around in Morocco and return to Portugal, he started to work on "Munchy 2".

I had seen Munchy 2 and all I could say was, good luck. Morocco? Phaah! No worries, mate! Mongolia, more like. This was going to be a beast. I would have to think about upgrading The Vespa to keep up with it.

# 18

## Reality

February 2010

## Reach

I had reached Tetouan. That meant I was going to be leaving Morocco soon. Should I stay there instead? I had heard the weather in Blighty was still awful. But I thought I had better meet up with Kev soon. We were kind of on this trip together and we were going to finish as we started, with me in a different time, place or reality than Kev.

I remembered leaving Portugal, with Kev on his C90. The first day we got split up. While riding through Spain, a journey I thought would only take us a couple of days, we arrived in most towns at different times of the day. I think it was pure luck that we occasionally arrived in the same town on the same day and sometimes even stayed in the same hotel.

But I was on my own. There is no more stopping on the roadside wondering where David Blaine has disappeared to. I missed the familiar sight of Kev's tool kit making a special guest appearance along the way.

I missed guessing which mechanic was working on poor Munchy.

## Hurl

I thought it fitting that I should stay in the same hotel we stayed in on our first day in Morocco, where we met Abdul a.k.a. - Terry the Tibbs Salvalez´ as the Essalam was full.

I still laughed to myself when I thought back to the time when we finally went through customs and actually got into Morocco. The fact that Munchy the Crunchy was still running and made it that far also raised a big smile. I also laughed at the fact that although I spoke to the half-blind hotel manager in Tetouan for some time when I first stayed there, he took a whole 24 hours to recognize me after I had returned. He recognized me in the same manner as he recognized which football team he watched on his small black and white TV in his tiny office, by quickly lifting his glasses, which were thicker than the air in the Marrakech Medina, and poking his beady eyes to within an inch of the T.V.

"Ah, yes! Charlie. How are you"? he excitedly asked.

As a welcoming drink, a kind offer of mint tea was quickly forced upon me. I did not want the half-drunk glass of tea he had been holding on to, which he handed to me. Being British, I thought it would be rather impolite to say no to a cup of tea.

However, a few of the other people at the hotel recognized me straight-away and kindly offered some home-cooked food that we shared from the same plate and drank some freshly made mint tea. They asked where the other guy (Kev) was. How they laughed when they found out he had to sell Munchy just to get home.

## Chuck

This time the hotel felt different. It was because it was full of young women. Full of the type of women who go out dancing in nightclubs at midnight, get some lonely sucker to buy them drinks all night, then return home at about 5 am and sleep all day. It's the. The only way... parasite.

No! That lonely sucker definitely was not me. I was too *careful* with my money, remember! I stayed for as long as I dared. I still did not want to catch the ferry so I decided to explore the coast, along the Moroccan side of the Mediterranean Sea in the east.

The road hugging the rocky coastline meant I rode south into the sun for a couple of hours. I stopped for tea in a lovely little coastal fishing village, stocked up on local supplies and headed back to the hotel in Tetouan, where I was keen to taste what I had just bought. This meant, in my mind, that I would need to stay a couple more days to finish off what I´d just bought, thus, it would prolong my holiday experience a little more. That was another time scale measuring device I had. I did not seem to go far whenever fresh supplies were abundant.

## Charlie

Kev sent me a telegraph to let me know he was heading back to Blighty soon, so I thought, right, I would catch the ferry back to Spain and I would do it soon. Ish.

I eventually left Tetouan at 11:00 am, again at a leisurely pace, stopping to take lots of photos, mainly of The Vespa, bought a ticket and caught the 12:30 pm ferry from Ceuta across the Straits of Gibraltar and was riding out of Algeciras port in Spain at around 1:30 pm.

As I attempted to get out of the actual port gates, I was shouted at by a Spanish official for doing another stupid U-turn on a dual carriageway.

"Welcome to Europe", I thought. I waved and smiled in Spanish, in the most innocent way I could think of and rode off.

## Brown

I hammered it all the way to Sevilla "a carrera tendida" - at full

speed.

This time there was no fuzz. No one could stop me now.

My get-me-home repair was still getting me home. I kept the throttle wide open for most of the way, stopping only for fuel for The Vespa and fuel for me (strong, fresh coffee).

Sevilla soon flew past.

Huelva was in sight.

Then I was in Portugal.

The sun was beginning to set. I wanted to reach the villa in Portugal before it was dark. Only because it seemed like a good challenge.

It took me about 5 hours. I worked out my average

speed was about 85 km/h, including quick stops for petrol etc.

If I looked at it in such a way that it took me just 7 hours in total, including the ferry, customs, petrol stops, photos, coffee etc., I worked out that I managed to leave my hotel in Morocco and arrive in Portugal in half the time it took Kev, who flew in a jumbo jet! (Of course, to make it sound fast, I did not include the fact that Kev left from Marrakech, approximately 640 km from the border. I departed from Tetouan, which was just 40km or so from the border).

Who said Vespas were slow? Well. OK. Uphill, The Vespa was quite slow if I did not take a ´run up´.

## Sugar

I still had not given The Vespa a nice name on this trip. ´Taj´, as in the Taj Mahal, was a contender since it sounded similar to 'Tagine' - a Moroccan dish that was hard to avoid. Which in turn made me think of 'tangerine' - the colour of The Vespa. I also noticed in the many photos I took that The Vespa had many different shades and hues of orange, bleeding into yellow, depending on what time of day it was, just like the Taj Mahal. I suspected most of the parts I had to replace when rebuilding it had been made in India. Lastly, The Vespa and the Taj Mahal both probably cost the same to build. The trouble was when I opened my mouth and called The Vespa, "Taj", it sounded a little limp, so I promptly dropped it.

Kev's input was, "Catnap".

I stuck to "The Vespa".

## Mick and Kif

So there we both were, together in sunny Portugal once again. Kev had been working on "Munchy 2" and I had been working on my sun tan.

I kept putting off the thought that I had, which was I still had another 2000km ride to get back to Blighty. I could not get a ferry until the 15th of February which meant Kev had to leave ahead of me, in his van, back through Spain and France to snowy Blighty, whereas I understood it, he was residing and dreaming of a "Munchy II". he seemed to work that it was cheaper for him to drive the long road back through France.

But there were already big plans afoot for the next trip. (The next trip?!)

A new bigger, better engine for Kev's crunchy would be on the way. I also had the technology to rebuild The Vespa. Gone were the days when I would pay a monkey a monkey to do a ´proper job´. Nobody had done that yet.

I had learned to do it myself. It was the best way. I believed Kev thought along those lines too. Those Moroccan mechanics had their fun and games.

Now it was our turn.

# 19

## Si si Espana si

El Torro - the bull

I left Portugal in search of Spain. I decided to head straight through the middle of the country. My dreams and wishes for a backwind, just for once, were not coming true. I would say, 90% of this trip has been riding into strong headwinds. If I ever got lost along the way, I would stick my wet finger in the air, check the direction of the wind and head in that direction.

Using the sun as a compass was of no use. I must have been turning into a vampire, as I had not seen my shadow since leaving Morocco. I dared not to look in the mirror either as my time scale had been ruined. I had not shaved when I needed to. For all I know it could be Easter already.

Wait a minute.

Was that an Easter egg I saw in the supermarket window? It was.

What day was it?

Where on Earth was I?

What had happened to the weather?

Where had my cloud landed?

## El Burro - the donkey

OK. I found out where I was. I was in a town called Friganal de Real, which seemed quite appropriate as I felt well and truly buggered after the fight I had with the wind, just to get there. I managed to ride about 200 km from the place I left in Portugal. And yes, it still rained.

Along straight open roads, I began battling with headwinds that once again slowed me down to 3rd gear. That was not the sunny adventure I thought about when I first envisioned the trip. I imagined riding in a T-shirt and shades, trying to look cool. But instead, I looked like I was the hair getting blown about by the hand dryer used to try and warm myself up during the quick fuel stops I made.

## Rein

The next stop was Caceres. I looked at the weather report before I left, and guess what. It was supposed to rain. When I awoke the next morning, guess what happened. It rained. All I could do was to put as many layers of clothes on as possible, just enough so that I could still move, take a deep breath and get on with it.

Staying positive, I thought that at least it was not as bad as the journey Kev and I had, from Fez to Ifrane. I will not forget that journey in a hurry but at least I could laugh about it. So looking on the bright side of things, I set off again for the next town. This time I planned to stop in a town that had more than 2 hotels and 3 bars. I felt quite young while I was drinking in one town as most of the regulars were either over 80 years old or the beer I was drinking had strange effects on my vision.

## Rain

The rain in Spain falls mainly on The Vespa.
Poor The Vespa.
I had made it to Caceres. When I arrived in town, I found an alarmingly expensive 1* hotel and dried my

things. And I mean I dried all my bits and bobs. I was wetter than a haddock's bathing costume.

When the rain finally stopped that afternoon, just as I entered my hotel room, I took a quick stroll through town in search of food. No food. It was Spain and, as it was about 4 in the afternoon, it was almost impossible to find somewhere to have a hot meal. I had forgotten the Spanish loved to fall asleep in the afternoons, waking up at around 9 pm and going out for food. I was not sure what people had to do during this siesta period if they wanted a hot meal. Personally, I had to survive on tapas and beer until any of the numerous restaurants opened. As I walked down a street, I picked up a familiar smell. Wait a minute I thought, is that lovely aroma coming from that bar?

I went inside to check it out. Inside I could no longer sense any sensimilla so I ordered a beer.

# Reign

As I sat there, I guessed that the aroma I had caught earlier was probably coming from the shop across the road, which I had noticed sold numerous items for growing exotic plants.

The few people inside the bar were getting drunk.

They were all under the age of 40. That was a good enough bar for me to sit and have a beer. The other bars I had been to earlier were full of `Spanish farmer idle chat´. This particular bar had loud music and drunken laughter. The barman, I found out, loved rock music. Oh well, not everybody is perfect. But he also loved Morocco and Moroccan things. He sparked up a lovely-smelling pipe in the bar. I was whole-heartedly encouraged to try it. I was most happy. He gave me some Moroccan souvenirs for my journey which made me forget about the fact that the Spanish played a strange game of darts. In that bar, they used weird, toy-like plastic darts and unfamiliar plastic dart boards. The game seemed like a version of ´Pin the Tail on the Burro´ but it made little sense to me. Who cared what the rules were. I joined in and we all enjoyed a few improvised games and got very drunk while doing so.

# King

The following morning, having been enlightened in the ways of Spanish darts, I decided to stay another day. I did not feel like doing too much with my hangover so tried to clear it with a walk around the beautiful little town of Caceres. I was glad I stayed a little longer to explore on two feet rather than two wheels. It made a pleasant change. What's more, I explored in glorious sunshine. Yes. I said 'Sun-she-ine'. It does exist after all. I was beginning to enjoy being outside again.

## Burger

What were you expecting? A picture of Elvis Presley? OK.

## Whopper

When I left Caceres, this time there was no rain. YIPPEE! Although the sun was trying its hardest to come out to play, the snow stopped it.
Yes. Snow. The first I had seen since the memorable stop in Ifrane, Morocco. Apart from that occasion, it was the first I had seen falling for years as I had often spent my previous winters in a warmer climate doing a similar thing, riding a Vespa through the mountains. I imagined people back home in the U.K., had probably had enough of the snow and cold weather. Well, me too even though I was in Spain. A place I often thought of as warm and sunny.

I headed north again towards Santander, where I had planned to catch the ferry back to Blighty. The only trouble was I had somehow managed to book a ferry that sails to Plymouth in Devon. I must have gotten confused between Portsmouth and Plymouth! Compared to Portsmouth, where we first sailed from when we began this trip, Plymouth was an extra 200+km away from home. That was almost double the distance. So close but yet, so far.

In a way, I was happy. It meant I could ride more. I did not want the trip to end. I wanted to continue to visit more countries. I was both mentally and physically prepared. I had always wanted to ride to India on a Vespa but when I seriously looked into it, I decided it was too expensive. That was one reason why I decided to go to Morocco. Somewhere with a different atmosphere to Europe, yet was a little more challenging. Part of that dream was to ride east across the top of Africa to the Middle East, but the borders were closed to enter Algeria from Morocco and had been for a long time. That was my lousy excuse anyway.

## Big Mac n' cheese

The next town I stopped at was Salamanca. No, it is not the place where James Bond villains reside but another interesting town where no cafes/restaurants were open until around 9 pm.

What did the locals do in the late afternoon if they got hungry? Well, I had to do something quite unexpected for me. Eat fast-food. The only place I could find in the whole town that sold anything warm (except small tapas) was a McDonald's. I still never went into that horrid place. Another walk around the block in search of something more appealing. I ended up heading for a Burger King that I had spotted in the distance. Not much different or better than McDoodoo admittedly but it was just enough to put me off wanting to eat anything else until 9 pm, when nice food was made available once more. My choice for dinner was either Asian or Spanish cuisine. I settled for a fake Chinese.

# 20

## From Dusk Till Dawn

### The Man with the Golden Gun

On the way out of Salamanca, I looked for the bar from the hit film, "From Dusk till Dawn", which Kev had mentioned before. Not the actual bar in the movie but a similarly strange place in the middle of nowhere with neon signs flaunting that a great time was to be had there.

Unfortunately, the snow, yes more snow, and the head-on winds, yes more head-on winds (and no, I was not making this up or exaggerating, the weather had been that bad) meant that I had not often lifted my head from the proximity of my speedometer, as the snow and wind would whistle down the back of my neck if I turned or raised my head too much.

So head down, holding on for dear life and gripping my handlebars like they were my wallet, I headed north into more bad weather. I thought one more stop off in a town before I would reach Santander, my final Spanish destination, would be OK as I still had two more days to travel 300 km. Under normal conditions, I had allowed an easy: 1 day = 250 - 300km, which was not hard to do. So, I took things easy. I did not allow for the gale-force winds, rain and snow, or getting chased off the roads by snow ploughs and could no longer feel the ends of my fingers or toes.

## Tula

I did not even reach my planned stopover town of Aguerilla. It was just too windy. I was forced, once again, to use 3rd gear for most of the way. I fell about 50 km short of, and about 2 hours past my planned stopping time. That meant that it took me about 6 hours to travel just 180km.

OK, so I did have to stop at every petrol station to warm my fingers under the hot air hand dryers in the toilets and drink copious amounts of steaming hot coffee to warm me up. I never stopped for long as I wanted to get to a warmer place as fast as possible. Portugal.

Whether it was uphill or downhill, 3rd gear was all The Vespa could manage. It was like being in the mountains of Chefchouan again, all those moons ago. I could not change the direction of the wind but I could change the direction I was heading. Not a great idea as that would have been an extravagant detour.

## Drag

I reached a place called Osorno. It had a choice of two hotels. One was as cold as the reception I got when I walked in. The other was a lot friendlier and the staff were very pleasant so naturally, I chose to stay there. I asked nicely if The Vespa could have its own room too, or rather, asked if it could be parked inside in the warm somewhere, out of the snow, away from wide-eyed Vespa snatchers, which it was. I ended up drinking a bottle of the house red to go with the dinner and the beers I had had that night. Once again, I had to wait until 9 pm for the chef to wake up but it was worth it in the end.

When I awoke the next morning, I ventured down to the bar area and thought I was still drunk. There, in front of me, were around 10 local guys and gals all in fancy dress. None of them spoke English, so I had no clue where they had been or what they had been doing. I knew they had been out all night, as opposed to going out that morning because the smell of alcohol was very prominent. The costumes they wore consisted of a couple of boxers, a man in drag - Napoleon Bonerhard and others dressed in such a way I could not make out what/who they were supposed to be.

While I was having my breakfast at the bar, scratching my head, wondering how or why I ended up in this scenario. An old local farmer came in and was immediately chatted up by the guy in drag. The old farmer was having none of it and promptly left, as he muttered in Spanish something about, 'that in his day men were men and..'. Probably. I followed him while I could escape the madness. I had to leave soon, otherwise, I would have been snowed in. Snowed in with the cast from a badly drawn cartoon wasn't my cup of tea.

# Retardation

As I looked outside, I saw cars half-covered in snow. "More snow", I thought.

When I went outside to retrieve The Vespa, I asked the guy at the garage if he had any skis that I could borrow, to help me get to Santander.

He told me, (I can't do the accent) "Normally, in a car, it would take about 2 hours..... and on The Vespa...", he said laughingly, "at least 4 hours".

"But in this weather...", I never heard how long he expected me to take on The Vespa as he was too busy trying to clear something from his throat. Either that or he was laughing too hard.

Once again, I shrugged my shoulders, found some skis for The Vespa and set off into the unknown.

'I may be gone for some time', I thought to myself.

Sometime it took too. I passed a whole fleet of snow ploughs, that ploughed majestically through the snow drifts of Extremadura. Along one particularly bad stretch of road, I stopped to take a few pictures of The Vespa in the snow drifts. I could not believe I was seeing. Neither could a guy who passed me in his 4x4 truck. He reversed back to me as he must have thought 'What the hell is this idiot doing out here on a Vespa in this weather'? and kindly asked if I was OK.

I was just trying to take a photo but my camera was frozen. Or my fingers were frozen. I was not sure which. Then the kind gentleman, in his nice warm 4x4 got out, with his camera, took a picture of me and said he would send it to me via email. What a nice chap. He also told me that it was -2 degrees. I was guessing that with the wind chill factor, it was a lot colder for me. I never did receive the photo he took. It must have been for his friends to laugh at. If you are reading this amigo, 'muchos gracias'.

A little further down the road, I stopped again to try and take a photo> Then, yet another 4x4 stopped with the driver asking if I was OK. Again, I said I had just stopped to take a photo. No one would believe that the roads were this bad. He got out of his nice warm 4x4 and very kindly took the photo for me.

What lovely, kind people they were in this neck of the deserted, snow-drifted, out-of-town area.

## Rise of the Idiots

On my 2x1, Santander was now in sight. The Vespa was going strong now that there were no headwinds and I was on the motorway doing over 113 km/h downhill according to the highly in-accurate speedometer.

I felt a strange sensation. There was no headwind. So that was what it felt like to have no head-on winds. I was so used to hearing the noise of wind rushing through my open-face crash helmet that I thought I had gone deaf when the wind changed direction as I could no longer hear that cold, freezing numbness which froze my ears. I thought about how nice The

Vespa sounded. It seemed to be going nice and smoothly, which boosted my confidence and spirit. Then, going through a 2.6km long tunnel, The Vespa started coughing and spluttering and almost stopped altogether.

No! Not now! I was almost in Santander. Please, at least let me make it to the ferry, I was so, so close. The Vespa spluttered and wheezed its way off the motorway and slowed down.

It did not stop completely.

It dared not. The Vespa may have decided not to start again if I stopped, so I just carried on at a slower pace. I had plenty of time to spare on my way to Santander.

I slowed down to around 80 km/h and watched everything on the road overtake me. Now I know how Kev must have felt cruising at such a speed all day. I´m guessing there was a fuel blockage. Or the spark plug needed changing. Or it may have been that The Vespa was so cold that it just wanted to stop and have a nice warm curry in a nice warm hotel. I pulled over somewhere safe and did the first thing all of us Vespa riders were taught, I removed the spark plug and cleaned it and set off again. The engine was a little noisy perhaps. Or maybe it sounded noisier because it was the first time I had heard the engine running at high speeds instead of hearing the head-on winds.

I would have been happy to make it to Plymouth, I

thought. Even if I had to push it off the ferry to the hotel that I pre-booked as I could not imagine riding home at 6 pm, towards Diss from Plymouth on a cold wintery evening.

## All-in-one

Yet, I was still in Spain, spending my last night in Santander. I spent it in a Cuban bar listening to salsa music and getting unintentionally drunk on the fact that my trip was just about over and I did not want it to end.

The next day I caught the ferry to Plymouth, where I would still have another 530 km to travel, to get back to sunny Diss. That journey would be the longest I would have made on this trip in one day. Although, it could have been the 1-day trip from Morocco to Portugal. The question was, do I do it one go or stop off halfway somewhere? All-in-one would be the answer of course. But would I even make it that far?

I had hoped that after all those kilometres, I would not need the assistance of a recovery service, which was a possibility, all the way there and back again. I was not covered for Europe or Morocco.

I was not sure The Vespa had recovered from the Spanish weather either but there was only one way to find out. That was to ride it full throttle all the way home.

# 21

# Homeward bound

I wish I wasn't

   I left the hotel in Plymouth at 9 am. That in itself was another shock to the system - 9 am. I was so used to sleeping and waking when I felt like it. To have to get up and move after hearing an alarm clock is not my idea of fun. The long lie down was getting shorter.
   The day started in traditional style with a traditional English breakfast followed by the traditional rain-clouds-a-looming. It wasn't long after I had set off that I started to loom along with the clouds and

consequently got very wet indeed.

Oh! How I missed the English weather. The sunny weather that is. At that time, it was raining and I didn't miss the rain.

## Stone the crows

Going through Somerset I noticed a familiar place name so I took a detour and went in search of a company I have been dealing with the previous year. My search and the detour took a lot longer than planned but the tea and company were worth the stop. Being able to dry my gloves out was also a huge bonus. Thanks, guys and gals.

I set off again, this time from Martock, Somerset at 1:45 pm. I thought I would have reached the M3 by that stage and it was already late. I had spent too long drinking tea. I needed to get a move on or I wouldn't be home until the next morning!

To help me along, the sun made a special guest appearance and later came out for an encore so it wasn't all bad.

## Stonehenge

Due to roadblocks, I had to take an even longer

detour and one particular road looked vaguely familiar. I realised I was in Pilton, home to the Glastonbury Festival. I had been there a few times before. Excellent!

Further on I passed Stonehenge and I didn't want to miss the chance of taking some photos, so I stopped briefly to take a quick picture of Japanese tourists taking Japanese photos of me and The Vespa.

## Like a rolling stone

The rain had stopped and the blue skies were trying their best to show themselves. Now that there were no headwinds the throttle was once
 again able to be held wide open.

Road signs with more familiar place names began to pass by and I was approaching the M25.

But no, not again.

The Vespa started to spit and sputter. It sounded like the same problem as the other day near Santander. I pulled off the motorway and decided that I wasn't going to ride like this for the 200 km or so that remained. It would have felt like Norman Wisdom giving Norman Collier a piggyback down a cobbled street, wearing stiletto shoes while eating a fiercely hot McApple pie.

# A stone's throw away

This time I quickly changed the spark plug and set off again regardless. I took out the hot spark plug and noticed there was a small deposit of carbon which was shorting out the spark plug, so I simply removed it and set off again, trouble-free, all the way home.

The only problem I had was that my little fingers were getting cold. I stopped to re-fuel, for the last time on this trip and I was told once again that it was -2 degrees. That probably had something to do with the numbness. It had rained so hard that my gloves and socks were soaked through which didn't exactly help but home was in sight.

That time no photos were being taken of me, and no happy, curious locals wondering what I was trying to achieve by venturing out in the rain, wind and snow. No fanfare to announce that I just covered a total of 10,000km on this little Italian hair dryer, all to get some Amlou paste, which, in the end, I had forgotten. Many people have ridden much further than me on Italian shopping bikes and so it is to all those I want to thank, for leading the way where others feared to go.

# Stoned again

I arrived back home, near Diss, Norfolk at 9:45 pm, feeling rather cold but the warm welcome was enough to put the smile back on my face after the trip I had just been on.

I laid The Vespa to rest for the night, maybe for the next few days, thanked it for the ride and had a nice cup of tea.

It was back to bed, back to reality, to dream of the next adventure.

Ciao.

Milton Keynes UK
Ingram Content Group UK Ltd.
UKHW021540021224
3327UKWH00060B/1917